Florida Historic Homes

Florida HISTORIC HOMES

BY LAURA STEWART & SUSANNE HUPP

ILLUSTRATIONS BY H. PATRICK REED

A guide to more than 65 notable dwellings open to the public.

A publication of The Orlando Sentinel
Sentinel Communications Company
Orlando/1988

Copyright © 1988
Sentinel Communications Company
633 N. Orange Ave., Orlando, Fla., 32801
All rights reserved

Edited by Rhonda Dickey
Designed by Katie Pelisek
Cover illustration by H. Patrick Reed
Illustrations by H. Patrick Reed
Maps by Peggy Alrich
Cover: Norment-Parry Inn, Orlando.

Printed in the United States

First edition September 1988

ISBN 0-941263-05-3 (paperback)
ISBN 0-941263-07-X (casebound)

THE AUTHORS

The authors of *Florida Historic Homes* work together at *The Orlando Sentinel*, and frequently discuss their ideas over lunch in the company cafeteria. Susanne Hupp is the newspaper's home design writer and Laura Stewart is its art and architecture critic.

Ms. Hupp was educated at the University of Missouri, where she studied English literature and journalism. She has lived in Orlando since 1962 and has written for the *Sentinel* since 1974. She has written about homes and preservation in Orlando since 1979. Ms. Hupp has three children.

Ms. Stewart studied at Barnard College, the University of Iowa and Cornell University. Her master's thesis was on 19th century American architecture, and she has been writing about art since 1981. She has been with the *Sentinel* since 1983, and currently teaches art history at Valencia Community College. Ms. Stewart has two children.

The two reporters decided to undertake the *Florida Historic Homes* project as a result of their stories on houses that have been renovated and restored. In researching the topic, they discovered that, while other states and many Florida cities have guides to the homes of noteworthy citizens and buildings of historic significance, the state of Florida had no overall list. They hope their efforts will add to an appreciation of the state's rich heritage.

DEDICATION

This book is dedicated to: those who planned their homes for Florida's unique climate and building materials; those who built for the ages, not for the moment; and those who protected and restored the state's old houses, and thus its legacy.

CONTENTS

CHAPTER I	The Heritage of Florida	5
CHAPTER II	The Old South: Florida's Panhandle	17
CHAPTER III	The Spanish Legacy: St. Augustine and Northeast Florida	41
CHAPTER IV	Steamboats and Citrus Groves: Central Florida	57
CHAPTER V	Sun and Sand: Florida's West Coast	73
CHAPTER VI	Tracks to Miami: Florida's Southeast Coast	89
CHAPTER VII	Treasures in the Tropics: Florida's Keys	113
FURTHER READING		125
INDEX		127

ACKNOWLEDGMENTS

Susanne Hupp and Laura Stewart are grateful to so many people for their contributions to *Florida Historic Homes* that it's impossible to thank them all.

But they would like to express appreciation to Florida history buff Nancy Taylor for her helpful suggestions, and to Sherry Davich, former director of Orlando Landmarks Defense Inc. in Orlando, for her advice as they undertook their research.

Florida Historic Homes could not have been written without such sources as Pat Fisher, Dr. Peck House historian; and park rangers Ralph Mallory and Jerome Bracewell of the Florida Department of Natural Resources, who answered endless questions about their "charges" — the state's historic house museums.

The authors also are grateful to the members of the many historical societies and organizations that saved the state's remarkable homes from decay and destruction, and also took the time to explain their complex histories and enthralling legends.

In addition, the authors appreciate the efforts of Dixie Lee Nims of the Florida State Division of Tourism, and Liz Ehrbar and Shari Naftzinger of the Department of Natural Resources, who furnished many of the photographs used in research for the book; Diana Jarvis, historic preservationist for Historic Pensacola Village, and Becky Roper Matkov, founding editor of *Preservation Today* in Miami.

Florida HISTORIC HOMES

The simple, homey Gilbert's Bar House of Refuge greeted shipwreck survivors.

INTRODUCTION

Better than history books and lectures, houses tell the stories of a place's past. They are where the pioneers and the politicians, the businessmen and their employees lived their private lives; they are the most personal of architecture.

Looking at houses — examining the size and materials and amount of ornamentation — also is a way of tracing a region's growth and sophistication. Houses — at least, the houses that survive the passage of time and problems of progress — show the native materials and local adaptations of styles. They show the changes their many owners have made to them as years went by and fortunes — too often — faded.

Houses, in short, show the human side of history. Old houses like those in *Florida Historic Homes* were built in simpler, quieter times. Most stood on large lots, in small towns, and were the proudest expressions of their owners' tastes and ambitions. Gradually, cities grew up around them and threatened their existence. Like the happy dwelling in *The Little House* by Virginia Lee Burton, most of the houses in this book have seen their share of ups and downs, and, almost miraculously, they stand today as proud testaments to our state's heritage.

In writing *Florida Historic Homes*, authors Susanne Hupp and Laura Stewart selected structures that were built to be residences. The buildings in this book are at least 50 years old and are open to the public, most as house museums. The others are restaurants or bed-and-breakfasts. They provide a cross section of the sorts of homes that Floridians lived in during the past 200 or so years of its nearly 500 years of European settlement.

Not all are the homes of wealthy people. Many of the homes that have survived are simple structures that belonged to pioneers who struggled in the state's often-difficult climate. All, however, offer insight into the history of a state that has seen some of the bloodiest wars and the strangest activities, from sheltering survivors of the state's many shipwrecks to building with the salvage of those shipwrecks. Better than any history book, Florida's old houses tell Florida's fascinating story.

CHAPTER I

THE HERITAGE OF FLORIDA

FLORIDA HISTORIC HOMES

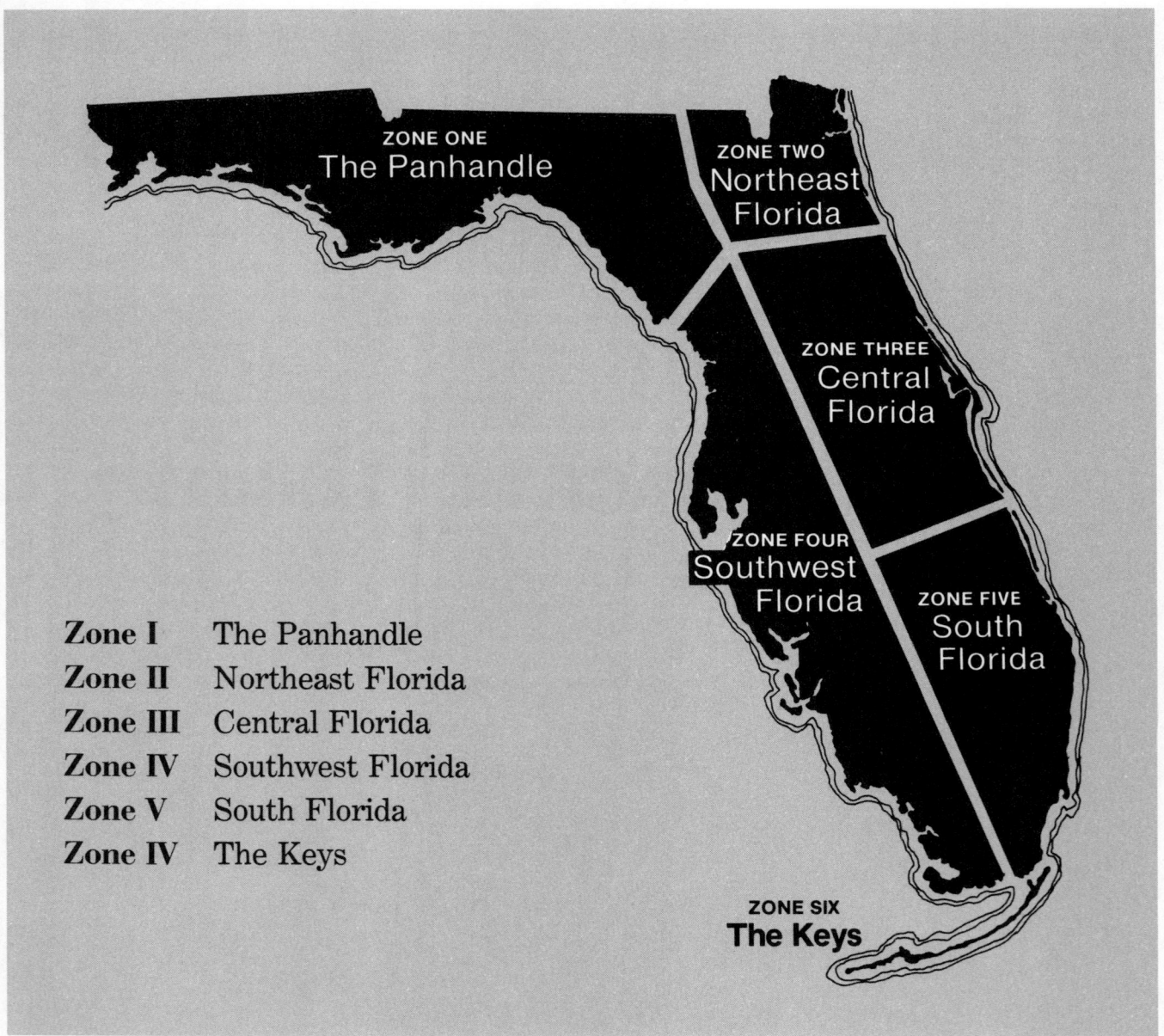

Zone I   The Panhandle
Zone II   Northeast Florida
Zone III   Central Florida
Zone IV   Southwest Florida
Zone V   South Florida
Zone IV   The Keys

THE HERITAGE OF FLORIDA

Land of Opportunity

Tall, glittering buildings dot Florida's rapidly growing city skylines, and eager visitors flock to its beaches and tourist attractions. Every day an estimated 800 people move to Florida, drawn by its sunshine and warmth, its groves and glades, and its promise and potential.

But, nearly invisible behind that booming reality stands another, older and equally intriguing Florida. It is a region that is surprisingly rich in history and legends. Many of its buildings stand as vivid testimony to its conglomeration of settlers. The architectural evidence stretches back well into prehistoric times — back nearly 4,000 years before Juan Ponce de Leon claimed Florida for Spain, naming it "pascua Florida" (feast of flowers) on April 2, 1513 for the religious holiday.

Long before it became *the* vacation spot for students on spring break and families seeking tourist attractions, long before Henry Plant and Henry Flagler built railroads through the state, long before high society wintered in Palm Beach, long before wreckers salvaged goods from ships in the Keys, before settlers and natives clashed in the Seminole Wars, even before Confederate leaders sought refuge as the South fell, Florida was the land of golden opportunity to a variety of newcomers.

And each of those newcomers, from conquistador to developer, has left a mark on Florida's architectural heritage.

The earliest known man-made

monuments, the mysterious shell circles found along the St. Johns River, were built by a long-vanished race known simply as the Ancient People. They, like the Indians who inhabited Florida as the centuries passed, probably lived in huts made of available material like wood and palm thatch. Spanish settlers later adapted this form of housing.

If early reports may be believed, however, the first dwellers built more than simple huts, shell circles and mounds. The Spaniard Hernando de Soto, who landed near Tampa Bay in 1539, painted a glowing picture of Florida's rich resources and architectural heritage. Immense, fantastic temples were decorated with shells, pearls and mica sand that caught the light and dazzled the eyes, according to one legend. Fabulous jewels and brightly dyed, painted and beaded garments were to be seen everywhere.

The earliest European dwellings were less glamorous, although their builders also made use of Florida's abundant natural materials. To defend their holdings from English plying the coasts and French Huguenots seeking safe haven from religious intolerance, the Spanish in 1565 established St. Augustine, the nation's first permanent European settlement.

It would be another century before construction began on the thick-walled Castillo de San Marcos, the oldest masonry building in America, but already a city was growing around the earlier wooden strongholds that had protected Florida's economic center. St. Augustine's earliest residents lived in "straw shelters," described by Franciscan monks as "wretched huts that scarce protect us from weather."

In the early days, houses made of wood and palm thatch or daub-and-wattle and palm thatch were common. Then, as the massive walls of the Castillo took shape — formed of coquina, a soft, pale local limestone containing broken coral and seashells — homes, too, began to be made of the material. The stone was held together by tabby, a primitive form of concrete made by mixing lime, crushed shells, sand and water.

Such early St. Augustine structures as the Oldest House, built before 1715, and the Dr. Peck House have solid coquina bases that provide protection from heat and hurricanes. Residences typically had balconies and wooden second stories made of hewn cedar. Roofs were thatched.

By 1763, when thriving St. Augustine's population had surpassed 3,000, Spain ceded Florida to England and most Spanish residents left the region. For nearly 20 years, Britain ruled a vast colony divided into eastern and western regions. St. Augustine was the capital of East Florida. Pensacola was the capital of West Florida, which was bounded by the Mississippi River to the west, the Apalachicola and Chattahoochee rivers to the east and approximately the 31st parallel to the north.

British rule lasted only 20 years, but it left an indelible imprint on Florida, modifying the dominant Spanish style of architecture and creating the well-ordered social systems and plantation economy that proved crucial for the state's growth. It was a period during which Florida changed considerably and its population became far more varied.

Debtors and beggars were recruited from Britain to help establish Rollestown, long since vanished, before moving to St. Augustine. Greek, Italian and Minorcan immigrants settled in New Smyrna. By the 1770s, when the Revolutionary War raged and England used a sympathetic Florida as a base of operations, 100 plantations were producing crops in East Florida that were very valuable to England — indigo, sugar, turpentine, citrus, tobacco and rice. For the most part, Floridians were British sympathizers who chose not to side with the 13 colonies.

As that struggle drew to a close and British defeat seemed certain, Florida's first land boom began. About 12,000 loyalists fled Georgia and the Carolinas, bringing their architectural traditions to Florida. Typical changes may be seen in St. Augustine, where homes were altered and expanded to suit their new owners' tastes, as well as to make them more comfortable during warm and damp seasons.

Flammable, perishable thatched roofs were replaced with durable wooden shakes and, to provide relief from heat and rain, early Florida rooms — called loggias — were added to many structures. Balconies, arches and stucco-style finishes remained, however, and the Spanish flavor was fixed in Florida.

In 1783, with Spain once again in control, another exodus of Florida residents began — this time of British loyalists to England, nearby colonies and the wilderness of the American West. But the English-inspired place names, boundaries, political systems, religious diversity, plantation economy and design developments did not leave with their creators.

Little by little, Spain permitted settlement of Florida by runaway slaves and citizens of the new United States. As the settlers became more restless and demanding under foreign rule, the region became difficult to hold. Fertile, prosperous Florida was an enticing region for the aggressive young nation, and after an overwhelming number of problems in the faraway colony — including land seizures and bloody incursions by America — Spain agreed to sell Florida. In 1819, Spain signed its unruly colony over to America for $5 million, which Spain never received. And two years later, after almost 300 years of Spanish rule, Florida became an American territory.

It would be another 24 years before Florida became a state, but those short decades saw tremendous changes in the territory. Hot-tempered Andrew Jackson, who had led two violent and illegal raids into Florida during Spanish domi-

The architectural influence of Spanish rule shows in the Ximenez-Fatio House.

FLORIDA HISTORIC HOMES

nation, ruled briefly as governor, and the division into eastern and western sections was eliminated. A new city midway between the capitals of East and West Florida, Tallahassee, became the capital in 1823.

Despite the suffering brought about by the seven-year Seminole Wars — fought as the remnants of a number of native tribes struggled to avoid deportation — the unified Florida flourished. Even before it attained statehood in 1845 with a population of 57,000, Florida had established an agrarian economy, and peace and prosperity allowed the construction of a number of gracious antebellum manor houses.

The land appealed to settlers as varied as Maj. Robert Gamble, who had established his sugar-cane plantation in Ellenton near Bradenton after fighting in the bloody Seminole Wars, and Prince Achille Murat, nephew of Napoleon Bonaparte and a planter drawn to Florida's promising future.

Gamble's mansion is typical of the period's style, with stately columns, broad verandas and use of indigenous materials — here, the familiar tabby — but it is the only one outside the Florida Panhandle still standing.

The Gamble mansion is a living reminder of Florida's antebellum past.

Bellevue, the simple frame home the prince built to replace his log cabin in Tallahassee, is less distinguished architecturally than Gamble's mansion, but it shows the practical, vernacular approach many took when building homes on new plantations.

Most were as unpretentious, though very likely as comfortable, as Live Oak Plantation, a two-storied frame structure built with wide, ground-level porches by Gov. John Branch before 1840. Like many of Florida's older historic homes, the Leon County residence no longer exists. It survived until 1894, when it was destroyed by fire, but many less ostentatious homes were dismantled around 1850 to be replaced by much grander versions.

Interestingly, one landowner who never developed his Tallahassee property was the famous French hero of the American Revolution, Gen. Marquis de Lafayette. Accused first of keeping his land off the market to increase its value, then of trying to sell it in lots for a greater profit, the impoverished aristocrat finally sold it piecemeal before dying in 1834. His dream had been to grow vines, olives and mulberry trees on the land, which would be worked by French peasants. He wanted to create a model community and help end slavery.

While an agricultural economy was evolving in Central and North Florida, the south end of the state was relatively undeveloped, except for Key West. Isolated from the mainland, the 2-mile-by-4-mile island had become the most populous city in Florida by 1850.

Its economy was far simpler than that in the North. Located on the hazardous but well-traveled Florida Straits, Key West became, in the 18th century, home to West Indian fishermen (traditionally called Conchs because of their fondness for the shellfish) and later to other residents and wreckers who salvaged goods from ships that came to grief on the Florida Reef. Although piracy was suppressed by the U.S. government after Florida became a territory in 1821, wrecking was still big business in Key West when the Civil War began.

Key West's unique wooden houses reflect Bahamian, New England, Creole and Victorian influences that together make up an indigenous architecture adapted to the tropics and inspired by ships' master carpenters.

Early Conch houses were built in styles similar to those seen along the New England seacoast or to those in the Conchs' native Bahamas.

Racy, raucous Key West was not typical of Florida, although the practicality of its architecture is typical of other indigenous residences that may still be seen throughout the state.

Built by small farmers and other new settlers, the so-called Frame Vernacular, or Cracker house, was made of split logs and raised off the ground for air circulation. Its roof was made of cypress shingles and was steeply pitched, allowing hot air to rise high above the heads of

A variety of influences shaped Key West's Oldest House.

FLORIDA HISTORIC HOMES

people in the house, leaving the living space cool.

During the early to mid-1800s, these log homes were almost identical in design.

Typically, two similar rooms were built under a common roof and separated by a breezeway called a dogtrot. Both rooms served as combination bedrooms, dens and sewing rooms. Wide front and back porches provided a living area and protected the house from the harsh summer sun. Meals were cooked and eaten in a detached kitchen some 20 to 30 feet behind the main house. The kitchen was kept separate so that if a fire started there, it would not spread to the rest of the house.

Later in the century, more modern Cracker houses were built of board and batten in prefabricated balloon-frame technique, so that they could be raised in large pieces and quickly assembled. The houses were roofed with metal, had high ceilings, and also had inside shutters to close out the hot midday sun.

Until the Civil War, Florida's culture and economy revolved around the plantation, yet the state never had many large estates. Most of the plantations the state did have

The Thursby House at Blue Spring recalls Central Florida's roots.

were in a huge arc curving from Jackson County through Marion County. About 80 plantations had more than 1,000 acres each; fewer than 50 had more than 100 slaves.

And, contrary to myths about the elegant way of life led by leisured landowners, few had time to develop an elevated, enlightened lifestyle. Most were too busy working their land and led surprisingly precarious existences. The Kingsley Plantation on Fort George Island north of Jacksonville, now a state park, serves as an example of the less-than-glamorous life on a Florida plantation. Yet even the smallest cotton farmer aspired to the grandeur that was associated with life on a plantation.

The truth is that Florida in the mid-19th century was still a rural, sparsely populated state. Before 1860, not one Florida town had more than 3,000 inhabitants. Yet Florida was growing quickly. In 1845, the population was an estimated 66,500. Fifteen years later, it had increased by 100 percent, and 12 new counties were carved out of earlier, general designations noted on maps.

When stirrings of the Civil War were felt in Florida, the state's economy and political alliances dictated its sympathies, which lay with the Confederacy. And with the coming of war, Florida found itself in a strategic position.

Federal arsenals in Florida were seized by Confederate troops in 1861, and soon after that all but three U.S. forts were taken by the South.

Approximately 15,000 Floridians served in the Confederate Army, but the state's greatest contributions to the war effort were material — Florida provided beef and other food to the blockaded South — as well as geographic. Its shoreline offered refuge to Confederate ships, while the Union's forts in the Keys and at Santa Rosa Island, near Pensacola, allowed warships to sail in search of Confederate blockade runners.

The state's tremendous productivity during the war brought it to the attention of the North, and Union forces fought to conquer the interior during the final years. In early 1865, a band of children, old men and a few soldiers held off Union forces at Natural Bridge in Tallahassee. They saved the capital.

In the end, the South fell and on May 10, 1865, federal forces entered Tallahassee unopposed. Florida's capital received the troops of occupation. Unlike its impoverished Southern neighbors, the state entered a prosperous era. Gone were the days of slavery and plantations; soon after the end of the War Between the States, Florida became a paradise for sportsmen, tourists and, particularly, for consumptives and other invalids.

A decade after the war ended, the great Southern poet Sidney Lanier traveled through Florida. In the guidebook he wrote, Lanier could barely contain his enthusiasm for the charms of the state. Lanier — like other vacationers, settlers and, increasingly, speculators — made some of his trip on trains, which jolted over track gauges, some of the trip by wagon and some by steamboat. It surely was an entertaining journey.

Some seasonal visitors to Florida, among them author Harriet Beecher Stowe, stayed in their own private homes in the state. The Stowes' was a lacily gabled, stick-style bungalow in Mandarin, on the St. Johns River near Jacksonville. (It no longer is standing.)

As the century ended, though, seasonal visitors were able to winter in sprawling, elaborate hotels such as the triple-towered, frame Sanford or the grand Ponce de

FLORIDA HISTORIC HOMES

Leon in St. Augustine. The Ponce de Leon was one of the nation's first poured-concrete structures and the first to revive the Spanish style. By the late 19th century, Henry Flagler and Henry Plant had opened Florida to widespread tourism by laying smooth train tracks over most of the state, and built spectacular hotels at each journey's end. In this eclectic era, any and every architectural style became the norm.

As tourism boomed, so did the state's population. Between 1860 and 1880, the population grew to almost 270,000, and included returning Union soldiers, visitors and planters, many of whom came from far away to enjoy society or to raise citrus — or to speculate on land.

Paradise had its down side, however.

A couple of cold days in the winter of 1894-95 changed Florida's history and gave rise to numerous legends. While guests enjoyed the amenities at Flagler's baronial Royal Poinciana Hotel in Palm Beach or Plant's Arabic/Moorish/Turkish Tampa Bay Hotel, the temperature outside dropped disastrously. Two successive freezes, one in December and the other in January, wiped out 90 percent of Florida's citrus crop.

According to legend, a group of British planters who had settled in Central Florida played polo while their trees froze, then packed up and returned to England. Those recent transplants were all second sons of wealthy Englishmen, who bought the land so that their sons would be suitably occupied. But, not understanding that such weather was unusual, the English growers left groves that once again bore fruit. More important, they also left homes built in the ornate, Victorian style that became part of the state's eclectic roster of historic buildings.

Another legend explains how Miami came about and a new section of Florida prospered.

Just after the second freeze of 1894-95, legend has it, Flagler was deeply concerned about the economy. Because of the freeze and the financial panic that had seized the country, his railroad had lost money. Surrounded by withered trees and faced with loss of revenue, he opened a box of fresh green branches abloom with orange blossoms — sent to him from Miami by Julia Tuttle. She was determined to show Flagler that the weather was fine farther south. Encouraged, he employed men to push the railroad almost as far south as it could go.

At the same time, Plant was pushing through on the west coast. He built the 600-room Hotel Belleview and its celebrated golf course in Clearwater. In addition, Florida's depressed economy was given a boost by the Spanish-American War of 1898, when troops were quartered in Tampa.

Residential architecture reflected the state's increased magnificence. "The Taj Mahal of America," Flagler's Whitehall in Palm Beach, opened in 1901. Like Newport, Lenox and other posh Northeastern resorts built by nouveau riche industrial barons, Florida was home to palatial surroundings for the Gilded Age's leisure class. These houses included opulent Whitehall and, soon after, James Deering's Villa Vizcaya in Miami, John Ringling's Ca'd'Zan in Sarasota, Addison Mizner's Spanish-style masterpieces in Palm Beach.

An influx of newcomers in the early 1900s brought the new Colonial revival styles and an elegant classicism to North and Central Florida. In the 1920s, yet another boom brought a taste for the exotic and romantic. Just before the 1926

THE HERITAGE OF FLORIDA

Henry Flagler's railway brought growth that reshaped South Florida.

hurricane, which practically leveled Miami, developers such as George Merrick and Glenn Curtis planned playful French, Italian, Chinese and Arabian Nights communities at Coral Gables, Hialeah and Opa-Locka in South Florida.

Addison Mizner's '20s Mediterranean designs in Palm Beach County, Miami's art deco houses and hotels of the 1930s and James Gamble Rogers' fanciful Central Florida homes added to an ever richer and more complex roster of historic residences in the state.

The backdrop for all this architectural experimentation is one of fairly constant growth. In 1880, Florida had consisted of a few coastal cities, vast agricultural holdings and the almost uninhabited — and, mostly, uninhabitable — South Florida. By 1920, the population had jumped from about a quarter of a million to a million. Six cities had more than 10,000 inhabitants; Jacksonville had almost 100,000. The residents of Tampa numbered 50,000 in 1920, while Miami was home to nearly 30,000. Once the coastal communities had been settled, people moved inland to the once-swampy Lake Okeechobee area.

By the mid-1920s, a railroad route linked Jacksonville to Miami, running through Central Florida to Palm Beach. By 1920, the state's 54,005 farms were valued at more than $330 million, and produced an annual income of more than $80 million. After the devastating 1894-95 freezes, farmers and planters diversified and citrus was grown farther south. And Florida again bounced back after the 1926 hurricane that hit Miami and then moved across Lake Okeechobee and on up the Gulf Coast, as well as the equally devastating hurricane that hit the eastern shores of Lake Okeechobee and the Palm Beach area two years later. The hurricanes, coupled with the 1929 stock market crash, temporarily put an end to the state's fabled land boom. But the forgiving land continued to produce, and its fine weather attracted winter-weary people eager to escape to an Eden that included amusing architecture.

Even the state's educational institutions mirror its varied, eclectic nature. Near the end of the 19th century, Florida's first major universities, Florida State University in Tallahassee and the University of Florida in Gainesville, were founded, along with such sectarian colleges as Rollins in Winter Park and Stetson in DeLand. The varied styles of the schools — turreted Romanesque at FSU, lofty Gothic at the University of Florida, Victorian Revival at Stetson and Spanish Renaissance at Rollins — are as colorful as those of the state's hotels and homes. Florida's other buildings are just as diverse, reflecting the state's rich cultural and architectural heritage.

CHAPTER II

THE PANHANDLE

FLORIDA HISTORIC HOMES

Zone I:
THE PANHANDLE

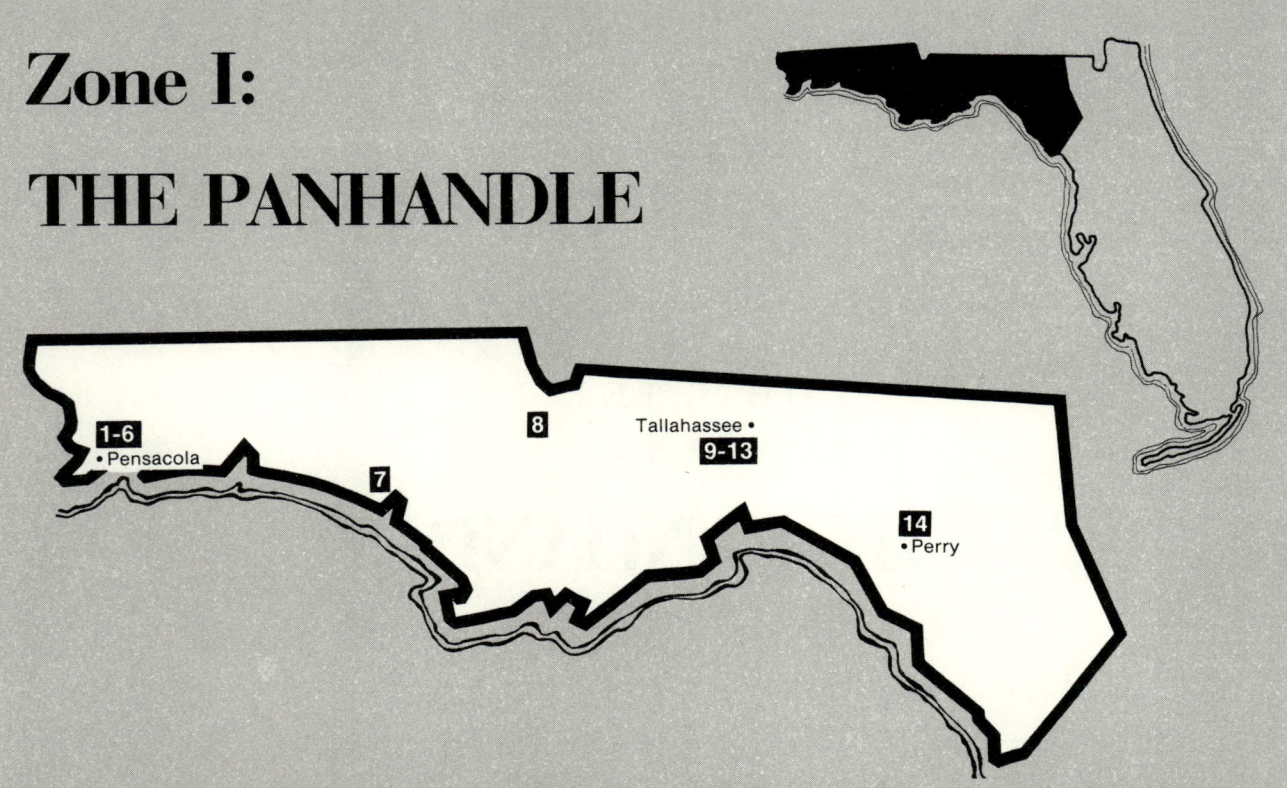

1. Quina House, Pensacola
2. Dorr House, Pensacola
3. Charles Lavalle House, Pensacola
4. Julee Cottage, Pensacola
5. Jamie's French Restaurant, Pensacola
6. Scotto's Ristorante Italiano, Pensacola
7. Eden House, Eden State Gardens
8. Gregory House, Torreya State Park
9. Alfred B. Maclay State Gardens, Tallahassee
10. Murat House, Tallahassee
11. Brokaw-McDougall House, Tallahassee
12. Beadel House, Tallahassee
13. The Columns, Tallahassee
14. Cracker House, Forest Capital State Park

The Old South

Early in the 16th century, when Spanish explorers first visited the hilly, timbered Panhandle, they found hostile Apalachee Indians already in residence. By the early 1630s, however, Spanish missionaries had established settlements in the region.

The Panhandle remained part of the crown's North American holdings for more than a century, until Spain ceded Florida to England in 1763. During that first period of Spanish domination, it's thought that missionaries lived in wattle-and-daub structures with palm-thatch roofs — thus adapted native materials and techniques to new uses.

While Tallahassee, Pensacola and other Panhandle towns were under Spanish domination, they were small, Catholic communities. But during the 20 years of British rule, from 1763 to 1783, the northern part of Florida was divided into the royal colonies of East and West Florida. It wasn't until the early 1800s, however, that the region began to show significant development.

Rapid settlement began in the fertile, 2,300-square-mile area in the northwest soon after Florida became a territory of the young United States in 1821. And in 1823, Tallahassee was chosen as the capital of the territory because of its location halfway between Pensacola and St. Augustine (the old capital cities of West and East Florida under the British).

Tallahassee, which the Spanish

missionaries had called San Luis, was given its name by Octavia Walton during territorial times. Daughter of a territorial governor and granddaughter of a signer of the Declaration of Independence, she chose a word that means "old town" in the Creek Indian tongue.

By 1824, when three log cabins were constructed to house Florida's Legislative Council, Tallahassee had been designed on a grid pattern, with Capital Square as the center. The first sale of lots was held in 1825. By the fall of that year, the town had 50 houses, seven stores, a church, a schoolhouse, an apothecary and a printing shop around the new square — and was incorporated as a city. It also had the first of many ambitious homes, and more would follow.

Tallahassee, with its nearby rich farming lands and potential for prosperity, attracted members of several wealthy Southern families. It also attracted the Marquis de Lafayette, a French hero of the Revolutionary War who never actually lived on his land, and Prince Achille Murat, a nephew of Napoleon Bonaparte who did settle in the state.

The city of Pensacola, far to the west in the Panhandle, was established in 1698 by the Spanish near the site of a colony that had been founded in 1559 by Tristan de Luna and abandoned two years later. It was in Pensacola that the transfer of the Floridas from Spain to the United States was arranged, and here that the capital of West Florida was established.

By the mid-19th century, the Panhandle was becoming a prime center for agriculture, particularly for cotton, as well as for the milling and shipping of lumber. Crackers — settlers from Mississippi, South Carolina, Virginia and Georgia — arrived to build humble frame houses or cottages that adapted the styles of the Gulf Coast and the inland South to the new climate.

Wealthy planters from other states moved to the region, along with their slaves and a taste for columned mansions and the porch-wrapped Gulf Coast and South Carolina Low Country plantations.

Florida's great Panhandle homes were raised from the ground to allow for maximum air circulation, as they were throughout the state. Verandas often stretched to two stories, providing shade from the subtropical sun and shelter from showers. And, like their counterparts elsewhere, Florida's plantations were built in such revivalistic styles as the Greek and bracketed Italianate.

The Civil War, however, destroyed the Southern way of life, and countless antebellum mansions fell into disrepair. After the war ended, many of the Panhandle's abandoned plantations were bought by Northerners for use as winter game preserves. The last two decades of the 19th century saw a shift from farming to hunting in Leon and Jefferson counties, and tremendous tracts of land were held by the new owners.

In the Panhandle, as in the rest of Florida, the amazing mix of architectural styles that may be seen in old houses reflects the history of the region.

QUINA HOUSE

The one-and-a-half-story, shingled frame cottage, built around 1821 by Desiderio Quina, is one of Pensacola's oldest houses still standing on the original site. Quina was a Genoan who had served as a soldier in the Spanish Louisiana Infantry Regiment. He came to Pensacola about 1814 and worked for Panton, Leslie and Co., a prosperous Indian trading company.

The house, which was constructed of local pine, cypress and oak and is raised on brick piers, has a double-fire-brick chimney in the center of its apron roof. The kitchen that is now attached to the rear of the house originally stood 7 feet behind the main structure. This was to keep both the heat of cooking and the threat of fire from the house. The kitchen replaced an open porch that matched the facade porch.

The porches on the rectangular building were recessed under gabled roofs and were supported by tapered columns capped with pseudo-Doric capitals. Ceilings and floors on the front porch are of strip wood. The porch is reached by walking up masonry steps of cement over brick.

Quina lived in the simple, five-room house with his wife, Margarite Bobe, and their six children. After Quina died in 1835, his family retained the house for another 32 years.

The house changed hands several times in the next nearly 100 years until, in 1966, it was bought by the Pensacola Historic Preservation Society and turned into a museum.

In 1983, the society refurbished it to the period before the Civil War, and included some memorabilia relating to Quina descendants.

The four-panel wooden interior doors are surrounded by simple wooden trim. Originally, the casement windows all had shutters. The house's two identical fireplaces have classically styled wooden mantelpieces and cast-iron fronts with arched openings.

Among the noteworthy furnishings in the house are a hair-cloth sofa and stool from about 1830, a square piano made in 1859, a pine Pembroke table from about 1820, a quilt made in the wandering Drunkard's Path pattern and a sleigh bed from about 1830.

The Quina House, 204 S. Alcaniz St., is part of Historic Pensacola Village. Admission is charged, and hours are 10 a.m. to 3:30 p.m. Monday through Saturday. For further information, call (904) 444-8905.

FLORIDA HISTORIC HOMES

DORR HOUSE

The two-story, Greek Revival-style house in Pensacola was built for Clara Barkley Dorr. She was a young widow in 1849 when she married Eben Walker Dorr. Clara and their six children moved into the new yellow pine house in 1871, the year after Dorr died. She lived there till 1895. Dorr was the son of Ebenezer Dorr, the last territorial marshal of West Florida and the first marshal of Escambia County when Florida became a state in 1845.

The house is considered significant also because it is a well-preserved example of Greek Revival architecture. The style, popular in the rest of the country early in the century, persisted along the Gulf Coast well after the Civil War, when home builders in the North had begun to adopt Gothic Revival and other late-Victorian styles.

Greek Revival decorative elements include dentil (or tooth-shaped) molding along the cornices of the building and the capitals of the columns. They, like the Greek-style fret meander that is on the bay window's cornice, show a fondness for the classical. Nonetheless, the house also is adapted to the climate: Its two-story porches shaded the house and permitted cooling breezes to flow through its high windows even on hot, rainy days. The home is raised above the ground on brick piers, and the lower part of the almost floor-to-ceiling windows on its facade may be opened like double doors to increase air circulation.

Its kitchen was added well after the family moved in. The house may originally have had a separate kitchen, or it may have been designed without a kitchen — for two years after moving into the house, Clara Dorr paid board to her sister, who lived nearby.

When the house was new, the walls of its ground-floor rooms — a hall, parlor and dining room — probably were papered. The upstairs rooms — a sewing room and two bedrooms — *may* have been papered. But it's likely that they were simply painted. The house's sawn-wood floors were covered, probably with ingrain or Brussels carpet, and there is a fireplace in every room.

After Clara Barkley Dorr moved out of the house in 1895, it served for a time as a residence and a private school, and from 1904 until 1952, it was owned by the Edward Miller family. The house then changed hands a number of times and was sold in 1965 to the Pensacola Heritage Foundation, which began restoration. It was purchased by the Historic Pensacola Preservation Board in 1975 and is maintained as a house museum. The house's furnishings evoke the period when it was new, although only one side chair, a straight-backed Renaissance Revival side chair, belonged to the Dorr family.

The Dorr House, 311 S. Adams St. in Pensacola, is part of Historic Pensacola Village. Hours are 10 a.m. to 3:30 p.m. Monday through Saturday. Admission is charged. For further information, call (904) 444-8905.

FLORIDA HISTORIC HOMES

CHARLES LAVALLE HOUSE

The four-room Lavalle House was constructed between 1803 and 1815 by Charles Lavalle, a Pensacola builder. Lavalle, who probably came to Pensacola from Louisiana, also was part owner of a brickyard on Gull Point.

The small Creole cottage resembles others in Pensacola known to have been built during the last Spanish occupation — as well as others built at that time along the Gulf Coast.

Its construction, however, was an unusual combination of brick and frame. The outer walls of the Lavalle House are made of beaded lap siding over brick. The interior walls were plaster over brick.

For the house's four-block move 20 years ago to its present site in Historic Pensacola Village, brick in three of the exterior walls and interior partitions was taken out and then reinstalled. One wall remained intact and is almost completely original, and even the original plaster remains on that wall. Floors are of random-width yellow pine.

Built on brick piers with a deeply recessed gallery porch under gabled roof, the one-and-a-half story house has four evenly spaced large doors on the front and back facades. Its steeply pitched roof is covered with cedar shingles, as it was when it was new. Two brick chimneys rise from the center of the roof.

The two front rooms adjoin each other; each opens into the identically sized room behind it, and fireplaces open into both rooms on each side of the house. One front room is now furnished as a bedroom, although it may have served as a main living room if, as is conjectured, two families occupied the house. A hidden stairway in one of the back rooms leads to an attic above that would have been used for sleeping and storage by the house's early owners.

Although it's likely that the original house had a separate kitchen, one of the back rooms now fills that role.

The furnishings — some acquired in recent years from private donors and others purchased from antiques dealers in Louisiana — are from the late 18th and early 19th century. A few of the pieces are of French origin, but the majority were probably made in rural Louisiana and elsewhere along the Gulf Coast.

The Lavalle House, 205 E. Church St. in Pensacola, is part of Historic Pensacola Village. Hours are 10 a.m. to 3:30 p.m. Monday through Saturday. An admission is charged. For further information, call (904) 444-8905.

JULEE COTTAGE

The simple, tin-roofed Julee Cottage was built in Pensacola between 1804 and 1808 as a functional, one-and-half-story house sided and shingled with cypress. It belonged to the legendary Julee Panton, a "free woman of color" who is said to have tried to purchase the freedom of her fellow, enslaved blacks and to have helped them in their new lives as freemen and freewomen. Such stories can't be proven, but Julee Panton is a symbol of courage and altruism nonetheless.

It is known that the small (about 27½ feet by 33 feet), rectangular dwelling was the first of several purchases of land Panton made in Pensacola. She later sold the property to another freewoman, Angelica, who went on to sell it to other black families.

Aside from its historical importance, the house is noteworthy because it is Pensacola's only surviving example of "to the sidewalk" construction. As such, it is reminiscent of the Creole cottages in the French Quarter of New Orleans. Traces of red paint may be seen on its weathered, patched siding, and it's assumed that each of the house's double-hung windows once had single shutters.

Originally, it stood with its narrow side parallel to Zaragoza Street, and was raised on brick piers to allow air to circulate below the building. The main, or east, entrance was reached by climbing a wooden staircase, and a porch and ramp were at the rear entrance.

Inside, two identical fireplaces stood back to back in two rooms, their wooden mantels featuring a simple classical design and their hearths made of concrete. The central chimney is of beige bricks, and has a flaring, corbeled cap. Crude stairs led to a loft. Floors throughout the house were of unpainted boards.

The house stood at 214 W. Zaragoza St. for more than a century and a half, until it was moved to 210 E. Zaragoza St. a decade ago. It was in ruinous condition when it was moved to its present location, and it has been rehabilitated to its original, early 19th-century appearance. It is used as a museum of black history.

Julee Cottage, 210 E. Zaragoza St., is part of Historic Pensacola Village. Hours are 10 a.m. to 3:30 p.m. Monday through Saturday. An admission is charged. For details, call (904) 444-8905.

FLORIDA HISTORIC HOMES

JAMIE'S FRENCH RESTAURANT

Pensacola's tiny, gingerbread-trimmed Jamie's French Restaurant is characteristic of the Victorian-style dwelling known as the Gulf Coast Cottage.

It was built in the early 1860s of native yellow pine and local brick, with large windows and high-ceilinged rooms opening off a center hall.

The cream-and-apricot cottage, constructed by attorney J.B. Jones a block from Pensacola Bay, stands on the site of an earlier Spanish settlement.

As was often the practice on the Gulf Coast at the time, the floor plan of the house was long and narrow to fit on long, narrow lots. Rooms were arranged one behind the other, railroad-car style, on either side of the hallway. The two bedrooms were opposite the parlor and dining room, and the kitchen was across the back.

The structure's hip roof extends over the broad porch, whose brackets and railing are decorated with cutwork trim.

The house retains its original two chimneys and four fireplaces — still the only means of heating the house — although the two bedrooms now serve as a large dining room with an open fireplace. Floors are of yellow pine planks and ceilings are of pine beadboard.

Restaurant owners Elizabeth Dasher and Gary Serafin have furnished the rooms in a flowery Victorian style with heavy walnut sideboards, Eastlake mirrors and lace curtains.

Jamie's French Restaurant, 424 Zaragosa St. in Pensacola, specializes in classic French cuisine. Lunch is served Tuesday through Saturday from 11:30 a.m. to 2:30 p.m. Dinner is served Monday through Saturday from 6 p.m. to 10 p.m. For further information, call (904) 432-5047.

THE PANHANDLE

SCOTTO'S RISTORANTE ITALIANO

Built in the 1860s, the small pink cottage that is now Scotto's Ristorante Italiano is typical of the late-19th century vernacular gulf coast style of architecture. Its boxy shape, open porch and ornamental brackets may be found in other older homes along the coast from Florida to Mississippi.

Tall double-hung front windows are sheltered from sun and rain by the broad porch, which is under a projecting hip roof. This arrangement allows breezes to circulate fresh air throughout. The foundation, raised above the ground, keeps the old building's floors dry and cool. To further provide cross-ventilation, each of the house-turned-restaurant's four rooms opens off a center hall. Sixteen-foot ceilings allow the warmest summer air to rise high above occupants' heads.

The white-shuttered, one-story house, which stands on Pensacola's historic Seville Square, has not been altered significantly. One of the original two chimneys that served all four rooms still stands. One room, possibly a kitchen house that was once separate from the main house, was attached to the main house at some point early in this century.

Richard and Pat Scotto established their restaurant in the house in 1984, and have furnished it to evoke the turn of the century with a little Victorian influence. Among its interior features are decoratively stenciled plaster walls, draperies in rose and burgundy, vintage photographs of the Scotto family, an old brass cash register, a hand-cranked Victrola, an antique etagere, chests and serving pieces.

Scotto's Ristorante Italiano, 300 S. Alcaniz St. in Pensacola, serves northern and southern Italian cuisine, specializing in seafood dishes. It is open for lunch Monday through Friday from 11:30 a.m. to 2 p.m.; and for dinner Monday through Saturday, 5:30 p.m. to 10 p.m. For further information, call (904) 434-1932.

FLORIDA HISTORIC HOMES

EDEN STATE GARDENS

The two-story, Greek Revival-style house at Eden State Gardens near Fort Walton Beach was built by lumber baron William Henry Wesley in 1896 for his bride, Katie Strickland. According to legend, it is a replica of an antebellum mansion Wesley stayed in while on the way home from the Civil War, and indeed it does resemble the well-known Dunleith in Natchez, Miss.

But the Wesley residence was, in fact, modeled after the Strickland family home, just down the street. It had eight rooms. The Wesleys needed all of them — they had nine children.

The rooms, in typical 19th century style, are of equal size and are arranged symmetrically on each floor. Two of the high-ceilinged rooms open off a central hall on each side of the house. In each room, four windows that stretch almost from floor to ceiling offer light and cooling cross-ventilation.

The house was built of native yellow pine, which was cut nearby and floated down the Choctawhatchee River, and stands on piers that protect the house from flooding and also increase the air circulation. The verandas show the adaptation of the Greek Revival style to Florida's climate.

When the Wesleys lived in their house, it stood in the midst of a busy lumber mill and outbuildings. Orange groves were planted so close to the house that the Wesley children could lean from the railing of the second-story porch and pick fruit. But a series of freezes killed the trees, the mill burned and, by the 1930s, the Wesleys had converted the upstairs bedrooms into apartments. In 1953, after the death of Katie Wesley, the property was bought by a retired real estate developer.

By the time Lois Maxon bought the house, in 1963, the vandalized structure was dilapidated. She renovated it, removing a wall between two ground-floor rooms and added air conditioning, indoor plumbing and the landscaped gardens that surround its centuries-old live oaks. Maxon named her mansion Eden and filled it with antiques, most from her family and some as old as the trees outside. Most of those pieces are still in the house.

She donated the property to the state in 1968. Among the house's highlights are the American Empire furniture in the library, the 17th century canopy bed in the Blue Room and the ornate Victorian bed in the Red Room.

Guided tours of Eden State Gardens, 4 miles east of the junction of U.S. Highways 98 and 331 in Point Washington, are conducted hourly between 9 a.m. and 4 p.m. Thursdays through Mondays. An admission is charged. For details, call (904) 231-4214.

FLORIDA HISTORIC HOMES

GREGORY HOUSE

The two-story Gregory House originally stood at the Ocheesee Landing on the Apalachicola River. It was built by planter Jason Gregory in 1849, not long after the territory became a state and the last Seminole War ended.

The clean, classical lines of the Greek Revival structure reflect the dominant style of the period more than they do the climate of Florida, although its shutters, cedar-shingled roof, interior chimneys and columned breezeway were practical features.

The eight-room house was built of yellow pine and cypress. It originally sat on 5-foot-high brick pillars to protect it from flooding, and overlooked a large lawn with two huge live oaks. The separate kitchen and dining room are connected by the covered walkway, and stand about 20 feet from the house. Other buildings on the original property were the warehouse on the river, a steamboat landing, a cotton gin and houses for slaves.

The primary crop produced by Gregory's extensive holdings was cotton, and the plantation was well-established by 1851. It prospered until the Civil War ended. Then the abolition of slavery toppled the South's slave-based economy and Gregory, like many other planters, went bankrupt.

He lost the entire plantation after the war, and moved with his family to Gainesville. Not long afterward, he was able to buy the plantation house back, and his youngest daughter lived in it from about 1900 until her death in 1916. After that, it stood neglected until 1935, when it was given to the state. It was dismantled in 1935 and moved over the next three years by the Civilian Conservation Corps to its present site in Torreya State Park.

The house is now decorated with furnishings that date from about 1800 to 1900. Among the historically significant pieces are the bedroom suite that belonged to Gregory's daughter and a variety of Victorian objects.

Like the house, the park site itself is historically significant. It was settled long ago by Indians. In 1818, Gen. Andrew Jackson crossed the river with troops here during an Indian uprising. And the first government road built after Florida became a territory in 1821 met the river at this point.

Tours of the Gregory House, in Torreya State Park near Route 2 in Bristol, are given at 11 a.m. and 2 p.m. weekdays, hourly from 9 a.m. to 4 p.m. weekends. An admission is charged. For further information, call (904) 643-2674.

FLORIDA HISTORIC HOMES

ALFRED B. MACLAY STATE GARDENS

The frame house in the vast, landscaped Alfred B. Maclay State Gardens was originally a hunting lodge. Built around 1909 by an earlier owner of the property, the 3,386-square-foot cypress house was renovated by Maclay, a wealthy New Yorker who had bought it in 1923 as a winter hideaway.

He worked on the house from 1923 to 1925. He put in such rare features as a birdseye-cypress-paneled library and a Tiffany leaded-glass lamp, and added two guest cottages.

The one-story Maclay house is of a simple, comfortable design that is well-suited to its climate and purpose. It is sited above Lake Hall, so that visitors see the lake across a vista of landscaped gardens. The roof curves upward slightly over the arch of the front door's fanlight, and wide side lights flank the door. To each side of the entrance are two casement windows with shutters. There are four fireplaces in the house.

Inside, the house appears today much as it did when it was occupied by Maclay and his wife, Louise. The library floor is made of 18-inch-wide, long-leaf yellow pine cut and milled on the property. A

large, part-silk Tabriz carpet lies on the pine planks. Among the room's furnishings are two Chippendale roundabout chairs from about 1770 and replicas of the Mycenaean Vaphio Cups.

In the living room are Chinese vases, an 18th century American blanket chest, Chinese metal paintings and an antique "Betty," or whaler's lamp. A Persian rug covers much of the floor, which is made of quarter-cut red oak and is made to look as if it had been pegged.

The furniture in the hallway and dining room also are antiques. Among them are a Hepplewhite mahogany half-rounded dining table with tapered legs, an Early American china cabinet made of cherry and pieces of 18th century American crockery. A bedroom has been converted into a gallery, in which interpretive exhibits on camellias and other plants that grow on the garden's 28 acres of formal gardens are shown.

During the winter months, when plants are continuously in bloom, the gardens are well worth visiting as well. As he worked on the house, Maclay began working on the gardens. His first effort, the Wall Garden, was created between 1923 and 1935, and features a 16th century della Robbia terra-cotta sculpture and two Italian cypresses. The reflection pool, constructed between 1935 and 1944, is lined on either side with tall sabal palms. A pond was built around 1943 to mirror the azalea beds on the hillside.

Maclay died in 1944. His wife, Louise, continued his work until 1953, when she gave the property to the state so that it could be maintained for the public as Maclay had envisioned them.

The Maclay house is open to visitors of the Alfred B. Maclay State Gardens, 3540 Thomasville Road in Tallahassee. An admission is charged. The gardens are open seven days a week January through April only from 9 a.m. to 5 p.m. For further information, call (904) 893-4232 or (904) 893-4455.

FLORIDA HISTORIC HOMES

MURAT HOUSE

The trim, one-and-a-half-story frame Murat House was the home of Catherine Willis Murat, widow of Prince Achille Murat. He was the exiled Prince of Naples and a nephew of Napoleon Bonaparte, and she was a grandniece of George Washington. During the second French Empire, after Murat's death, Catherine Murat was officially recognized as a princess and given financial assistance by Napoleon III, whose court she visited. Yet the Murat house is a humble one.

Murat's widow purchased the house in 1854. She called the house Bellevue — French for "lovely vista" — and lived in it until her death in 1867. It originally sat on 520 acres about 2 miles west of Tallahassee on the Jackson Bluff Road.

The Murat house was moved to its present location in southwest Tallahassee in 1967, and its interior was restored to the period when the princess lived there. It is furnished with such mid-19th century pieces as a washstand with ewer and basin in the bedroom, a late Empire-style pier table in the hallway and a Hepplewhite corner cabinet in the parlor.

The frame structure shows the fine adjustment of Florida vernacular architecture to its environment and climate. Chimneys rise from each end of the cottage, which has porches on each facade. Those porches are covered by the roof, which projects over the open sections of the house. The house itself is raised above the ground on brick piers. Tall windows on three sides of the house offer cross-ventilation, and the steep pitch of the shingled roof allows hot air to rise to the top of the ceiling, leaving the lower part of the house cool.

The Murat House is on the grounds of the Tallahassee Junior Museum at 3945 Museum Drive in Tallahassee. Hours are 9 a.m. to 5 p.m. Tuesday through Saturday, 12:30-5 p.m. Sunday. An admission is charged. For further information, call (904) 575-8684.

BROKAW-McDOUGALL HOUSE

When Peres Bonney Brokaw arrived in Tallahassee in 1840, he was young and unmarried. He had moved from New Jersey to Alabama and then, in the late 1830s, to Florida, where he went into the livery business and prospered. In 1850, he married. Six years later, as his family grew, he began constructing the Italianate, two-story mansion that would stand as one of the few of its type.

By 1860, the clapboard house — which had overhanging eaves and a broad front porch supported by six Corinthian columns — was complete, as was the landscaping on Brokaw's property. Four live oak trees, like the camellias and other plantings in the gardens, all date from the period when the house was new.

Brokaw died in 1875, and the house went to his daughter Phoebe, who had married a recent Scottish immigrant, Alexander McDougall. Phoebe died in 1883, and McDougall married her sister Eliza. The house remained in the family until 1973, when the descendants of the original owners gave it to the state of Florida.

The eight-room house, which is the home of the Tallahassee Preservation Board, has been completely restored to the style of the mid- to late 19th century. The gardens were restored in 1976 as a bicentennial project of the Florida Federation of Garden Clubs and the Tallahassee Preservation Board.

Shutters hang on large casement windows on the house, which recently was repainted in its 1884 colors — Tuscan yellow with green and brown trim. A graceful balustrade surrounds the veranda on the second story. Each of the symmetrically arranged rooms, which open off a long hall, has a high ceiling.

The square plan culminates in a square cupola at the center of the peaked, shingled roof. Trim brackets project from the wide eaves, punctuating the house's proportions and adding a decorative element.

Interior features include a high ceiling and large halls running the length of both floors. The rooms on either side of both upstairs and downstairs hallways are identical in size. On the first floor, they are separated by bathrooms that were originally used for storing trunks. Several rooms are furnished in the style of the period when the house was new.

The Brokaw-McDougall House, 329 North Meridian in Tallahassee, is open Mondays through Fridays from 8 a.m. to 5 p.m. There is no admission charge. For further information, call (904) 488-3901.

FLORIDA HISTORIC HOMES

BEADEL HOUSE

The two-story frame house at Tall Timbers Research Station near Tallahassee represents an important period in Panhandle history. The house was developed and used when vast areas that had been plantations were occupied by Northerners who hunted quails.

The original section of the house was built around 1895 by Edward Beadel, a New York architect who was independently wealthy and who came South every winter to hunt. He had purchased the land from the owners of a larger estate in the Florida red hills, the Live Oak Plantation, and had named the estate Tall Timbers.

Its second owner, Henry Beadel (Edward's nephew), was a naturalist and philanthropist who left his entire estate to be used as an ecological research station. He was one of the pioneers in the use of firs as a land management tool for quail propagation, and also was a noted nature photographer. The house he and his uncle Edward lived in is now used as administrative offices and living quarters for visiting scholars to Tall Timbers.

Henry had visited Leon County every winter until 1919, when he inherited Tall Timbers and became a permanent resident of Florida. The younger Beadel added a one-story, five-bay wing to the east of the older building in 1921, retaining the pleasant Vernacular Colonial Revival style and linking the two buildings with an 86-foot-long porch framed with square posts, wooden balustrade and wisteria trellis. A three-bay dormer was constructed in the old shingled roof to add more bedroom space.

The original two-story section is a rectangular building with a gabled roof that was probably designed by Edward Beadel and built for $3,000 by a Thomasville contractor. There are four rooms on each floor, which is divided by a central hall and joined by a U-shaped staircase to the rear.

Painted yellow with white trim, like the main house, the 1921 addition has a master bedroom, bathroom and a large living room/study. The main house was modernized when it was converted into the Tall Timbers Research Station, although the wainscoting in its rooms and halls has been preserved. But the addition has been kept as it was when Henry Beadel lived in it, from 1921 to 1963.

The living room/study is a museum that contains books, photographic equipment and tools used for research and collecting by Henry Beadel. The room is paneled in brown sweet gum wood. Heavy oak beams support its 12-foot-high ceiling. A 7-foot-wide fireplace dominates the north wall of the 36-by-40-foot room, and mounted fish and beehives hang from the walls.

The house is set on brick piers with cinder-block infill, on a slope facing Lake Iamonia, screened by live oaks and magnolias. An 1890s photo shows it with a huge front lawn, landscaped with native grasses and framed by pines and hardwood trees. Photos from early in the 20th century show the house with a picket fence, planted flowers, a vegetable garden and imported palm trees. Today, an open vista with minimal plantings is maintained at the house. The economy that produced the residence, first a plantation and later a hunting preserve, is gone. But the house stands as a reminder of those days.

The Beadel House, Tall Timbers Research Station on Route 1 near Tallahassee, is open Monday through Friday from 8 a.m. to 4 p.m. No admission is charged. For further information, call (904) 893-4153.

FLORIDA HISTORIC HOMES

THE COLUMNS

The oldest surviving house in Tallahassee, The Columns was begun in 1830 for banker William Williams, his wife and their 10 children. The three-story brick mansion was designed with an attached, two-story ell and keynote columns supporting a two-story, pedimented porch.

The Williamses moved back to Georgia in 1833, however, and for 10 years their house was owned by and operated as a bank. During the 1840s, banking in the state collapsed and the house was sold at a sheriff's sale in 1847 to satisfy creditors.

Eventually, the house became Mrs. Demilly's Boarding House. The structure was poorly maintained until after the Civil War, when Dr. Alexander Hawkins purchased it. He lived and conducted his practice in the porticoed, Greek Revival house for more than 20 years. In 1897, it was bought by Thomas J. Roberts, one of Leon County's most successful post-war planters, for his young wife. She gave the already venerable house its name.

In 1907, The Columns was extensively restored. Almost a century old, it retained its residential character until 1925. Then, in the hands of real estate dealers, it became a center of business activity. Its basement became offices, and the upper floors apartments. One of the best-known of its tenants was the Dutch Kitchen, a tearoom that occupied the basement from 1925 to 1956.

The Columns was sold to the First Baptist Church in 1956, and in 1970 the church offered the building to anyone who would move it. The next year, the old house was moved to another downtown location, and was renovated to serve as the headquarters of the Tallahassee Area Chamber of Commerce.

Its exterior appearance has been retained, and some rooms are furnished in a period style. The entrance hall and reception room feature antiques from about 1830 to 1845, among them the Empire mahogany mirror and the French Restoration pier table. Over a red velvet sofa in the reception area is a portrait of Mrs. Benjamin Chaires, an early resident of The Columns, and other small pictures in the room are hand-colored engravings that date from 1790 to 1817. The board room contains two authentic late Empire chests, and a large banquet table and 12 chairs in the Hepplewhite style.

The Columns, 100 N. Duval St. in Tallahassee, is open 8:30 a.m. to 5 p.m., Monday through Friday. No admission is charged. For further information, call (904) 224-8116.

THE PANHANDLE

CRACKER HOUSE

The restored pioneer Cracker House is similar to many houses built in the Panhandle soon after Florida became a territory in the early 19th century.

Settlers moved south from South Carolina, Virginia and Georgia. Those newcomers came in ox-drawn wagons, cracking their whips over the heads of their animals and, according to legend, were dubbed Crackers. Unable to build with their accustomed clay, they adapted their building styles to a new material — the abundant lumber they found in North Florida.

A typical Cracker house, this one-story cabin in Forest Capital State Park near Perry was built around 1863 by Wiley Washington Whiddon. It was made with double-notched square logs cut from his land.

The house is 60 feet long and consists of four rooms — a living room and a kitchen/dining room separated by a breezeway (called a dogtrot) and two bedrooms, one for boys and one for girls, that were added later.

The house's shake shingles were made from cedar, and its longer beams were lap-jointed and held together with wooden pegs. A wooden fence surrounded this pioneer home, keeping the chickens in and foxes and other predators out. The yard was always carefully raked so the occupants could see snakes more readily, and to protect against fire. Porches on both sides of the building offered shade and shelter from showers, allowing the large windows to be kept open to admit breezes. The house was raised from

the ground so that cooling air could flow beneath it.

All rooms in the Cracker House have fireplaces with chimneys made of fieldstone and homemade mortar. The house has such period furnishings as mosquito netting that flows from the ceiling in a pyramid over the bed, simple chairs and tables and, outside, a cane grinder and a hand-wringer. Also on the grounds are a vineyard, stable, henhouse and a general-purpose shed.

The Cracker House, at the Forest Capital State Museum, is about a mile south of Perry on U.S. Highways 27 and 19. The park is open 9 to noon and 1 to 5 p.m. Thursday through Monday. An admission is charged. For further information, call (904) 584-3227.

CHAPTER III

NORTHEAST FLORIDA

FLORIDA HISTORIC HOMES

Zone II:
NORTHEAST FLORIDA

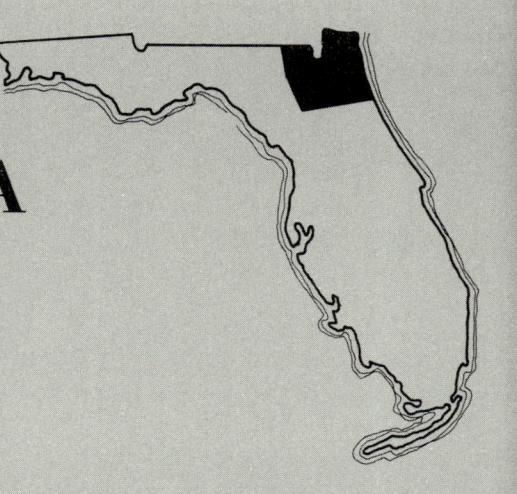

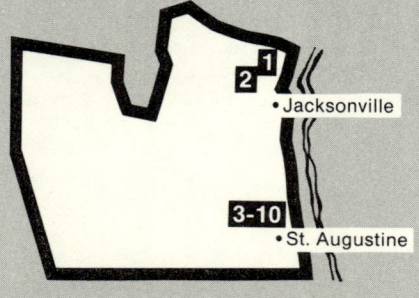

1. Bailey House, Fernandina Beach
2. Kingsley Plantation, Fort George Island
3. Oldest House (Gonzales-Alvarez), St. Augustine
4. Wescott House, St. Augustine
5. Fernandez-Llambias House, St. Augustine
6. Ximenez-Fatio House, St. Augustine
7. Dr. Peck House, St. Augustine
8. Raintree Restaurant, St. Augustine
9. Casa De Solano, St. Augustine
10. Victorian House, St. Augustine

NORTHEAST FLORIDA

The Spanish Legacy

Although English and American influences can be found in the historic buildings of northeastern Florida, the dominant early influence was Spanish.

That's hardly surprising, because the first Spanish explorers to set foot in the new colony, Pascua Florida, did so somewhere near present-day Ponte Vedra Beach, south of Jacksonville Beach, in 1513. The Spanish dominated the region for centuries.

When Pedro Menendez de Aviles established St. Augustine, in 1565, he and his men probably built dwellings like those of the Indians in the area — using palm thatch and wood, or perhaps wattle and daub. They built a series of log forts to defend their settlement until the late 17th century, when work began on the sturdy, thick-walled Castillo de San Marcos. Local coquina stone was the building material.

When construction began on the fort in 1672, residents of St. Augustine also began using coquina or a combination of coquina stone and tabby — a primitive mortar made of crushed shells, limestone, sand and water — on their homes. Most houses, however, still were made of wood.

Many of the town's more perishable wooden houses were destroyed in 1702, when English colonists from the Carolinas attacked St. Augustine. In the building boom that followed, the Spanish settlers built houses that were more permanent and fireproof. By 1763, when

Spain ceded Florida to England in the Treaty of Paris, St. Augustine was a bustling town with 3,000 inhabitants and a number of stone, or stone-and-wood, houses.

The new British inhabitants of St. Augustine, in need of firewood, tore down many of the flimsy, wooden structures and expanded the existing stone structures. They usually added fireplaces to rooms formerly warmed by braziers, and glass to windows that had been shuttered or latticed, but not glazed. British occupation lasted only 20 years, but the improvements during that time endured and created a unique architectural style still seen throughout the Ancient City.

Prosperity came to the region in the early years of the 19th century, when Florida became first a territory and then a state. By midcentury, St. Augustine was a thriving community. The arrival of a honeymooning Henry Flagler in 1883 increased its popularity among winter tourists, many of them invalids eager to rest quietly among the city's fragrant gardens and groves. They came South and stayed all winter at hotels like that operated by Louisa Maria Philipa Fatio.

During the 1880s, however, Flagler determined that he would make the area a booming resort. He built the grand Ponce de Leon Hotel and the nearby Alcazar, and acquired and renovated the Cordova. He provided the town easy access with the rest of the nation by rail.

Within little more than a decade of the opening of the Ponce de Leon, Flagler and his fashionable tourists moved on to the more stylish Palm Beach, and then on to warmer Miami. St. Augustine and neighboring cities grew gradually, and never failed to attract sightseers and visitors.

NORTHEAST FLORIDA

BAILEY HOUSE

The Victorian Bailey House in Fernandina Beach, now a bed-and-breakfast inn, was built in 1895 for Effingham W. Bailey, an agent for a shipping company, and his bride. Their architect was George W. Barber of Knoxville, Tenn., designer of many fashionable Florida homes.

The lot the house stands on was a wedding gift. Legend has it that the young Mrs. Bailey had a choice: She could have a modest home with luxurious furnishings, or she could have a lavish home that would be furnished as the couple could afford it.

Clearly, Mrs. Bailey chose the second option.

The richly detailed, Queen Anne-style home — with wraparound porches on the ground level and romantic bay windows on all three levels — is a grand house. It took three years to build and cost a then-outrageous $10,000. Two turrets and steep gables add dramatic accents to its skyline silhouette, and brackets ornament its eaves. Lacy scrollwork brackets rise above the turned columns of the porch, above the trim balustrade.

Inside, the house, which stayed in the Bailey family until 1963, is equally ornate. Over the spectacular fireplace in the reception hall is an inscription: "Hearth Hall, Welcome All." The stained-glass windows in the entrance area are in the Tiffany style that was popular at the turn of the century.

Most of the furnishings at the inn are American antiques that evoke a sense of the period, and include marble-topped tables, brass beds, pump organs, fringed lamps and claw-footed bathtubs. In addition, there are five other fireplaces in the bedrooms.

The Bailey House is at 28 7th St. S. in Fernandina Beach. Room rates vary. For further information, call (904) 261-5390.

FLORIDA HISTORIC HOMES

NORTHEAST FLORIDA

KINGSLEY PLANTATION

The state's oldest surviving plantation was begun by John McQueen in 1791. McQueen had received the plantation's site, Fort George Island near Jacksonville, from the king of Spain that year, and built its first house. That house is now known as the Kitchen House.

The plantation's second owner, John Houston McIntosh, purchased it in 1804. But McIntosh left the area after falling into disfavor with the Spanish because he had joined an attempt to overthrow the government.

In 1812, Zephaniah Kingsley moved into the small house, and five years later foreclosed on the property. He bought it for $7,000 and built himself the large, frame manor house that is now one noteworthy structure on the plantation.

A wealthy and learned man, Kingsley would become a member of the Second Legislative Council of the Territory of Florida under President James Monroe. He advocated the lenient treatment of slaves, but also considered slavery the best way of ensuring agricultural success in the South. Kingsley raised Sea Island cotton, sugar cane and other cash crops on his approximately 1,100-acre plantation, shipping them to Savannah and Charleston for sale.

His slaves — who numbered as many as 1,500 at some times and as few as 200 at others — also grew orange trees, rice and vegetables on the plantation. And they raised livestock, fished in the plantation's waters and hunted on its less-developed sections.

Kingsley's nephew, Kingsley Beatty Gibbs, took over management of the plantation in 1836, and lived in the house. But until the period after the Civil War, when the house was sold to John Rollins, Kingsley Plantation had a great many owners. Rollins remodeled the by-then ancient Kitchen House and the main house, and added two rooms, bay windows and inside stairways. He also removed fireplaces, though the reason for that is not known.

Among the plantation buildings still standing are the Kingsley manor house, the smaller McQueen (or Kitchen) House, a tabby barn built in 1791, and one of the 32 slave cabins.

The two-story, pine and brick Kingsley manor house contains seven rooms and a hallway downstairs, and Kingsley's bedroom and office upstairs. The deep porch on the facade of the raised house is flanked by shingled, hip roofs, and above the porch is a three-bay second story. The house's tall casement windows were added by Rollins, replacing small glazed windows with shutters so that as much air as possible could circulate through the house.

Among the house's furnishings are items that belonged to Gibbs and Rollins, including a collection of the latter's books. Other furnishings include objects dating from the 1830s to the post-Civil War Victorian styles. Carpets and draperies are copies of those used in the mid-19th century, long after the period when Kingsley first lived in the grand old plantation.

The Kingsley Plantation is on Fort George Island, 14 miles east of Jacksonville off State Road A1A. The plantation grounds are open from 8 a.m. to 5 p.m. daily. An admission is charged for tours, which are scheduled Thursdays through Mondays. For further information, call (904) 251-3122.

FLORIDA HISTORIC HOMES

ST. AUGUSTINE'S OLDEST HOUSE

The two-story, shingled structure in the Ancient City shows several influences. The present house stands on the site of a much older, more primitive dwelling, probably a board-and-thatch hut built in the 1600s and burned during the invasion of British troops in 1702.

By the early 1700s, the current house, then a one-story structure, had been built to take the place of the more perishable hut. This house is of coquina stone, a native shellstone quarried on nearby Anastasia Island, and tabby, a mortar made of sand, crushed shells and water. The house was occupied by Tomas Gonzalez y Hernandez, a Canary Island immigrant who was an artilleryman at the Castillo de San Marcos.

It's thought that he might have acquired it through his marriage in 1723. During this time, the house gained a clapboard second story. The family lived in the house until 1763, when Spain gave Florida to Great Britain and most Spanish inhabitants of St. Augustine moved to Cuba.

The Hernandez house became the property of Maj. Joseph Peavett, the paymaster for the English military. The house was changed still further. Glass panes replaced the latticework in its windows, and fireplaces were added. After Peavett's death, his widow lived there for a time with her new husband, a gambler whose debts finally forced her to sell her home at auction in 1790. It was purchased by Geronimo Alvarez, a Spaniard, and was his family's home for almost a century.

The house became the headquarters of the St. Augustine Historical Society in 1918, and was restored to its late-18th century appearance. A roofed balcony projects from one end of the structure, and cypress-shake shingles cover its hip roof.

Inside, some of the rooms are furnished in the plain Spanish furnishings of 1600s and 1700s, while others show the influence of later styles. Maria Peavett's room reflects the time it was used — the late 18th century. The bed of Gen. Hernandez, a leader in the last Seminole War, may be seen in one bedroom, which is furnished in the style of the early American territorial period.

The kitchen, in the style so typical of Spanish buildings and hot-climate dwellings, occupied a separate building to reduce the danger of fire and to keep cooking odors out of the main house.

St. Augustine's Oldest House, 14 St. Francis St., is open 9 a.m. to 5 p.m. every day except Christmas. Last tour begins at 4:30 p.m. An admission is charged. For further information, call (904) 824-2872.

NORTHEAST FLORIDA

WESTCOTT HOUSE

The Victorian, clapboard Westcott House in St. Augustine was built in the late 1880s for Dr. John Westcott. He was involved in the development of the St. Johns Railroad and the Intracoastal Waterway.

In 1983, it was converted into a bed-and-breakfast inn. The house has porches on its first and second stories facing the street, and a smaller, first-level porch around a projecting bay on the side of the house. Its double front door is to the left of the symmetrical facade. The other two bays contain large casement windows. Delicate scrollwork brackets ornament the wide eaves, their graceful lines echoing those of the scrollwork brackets on the porch's square columns.

The Westcott House is raised on piers to protect it from flooding and to permit cooling breezes to circulate below. The deep porches and tall windows also allow the house to take full advantage of the subtropical climate's every breeze; the windows are shaded by the porch and sheltered from storms.

The house is in St. Augustine's Historic District, overlooking Matanzas Bay and the Bridge of Lions.

The Westcott House is at 146 Avenida Menendez in St. Augustine. Rooms rates vary at the bed-and-breakfast. For further information, call (904) 824-4301.

FLORIDA HISTORIC HOMES

FERNANDEZ-LLAMBIAS HOUSE

The two-story, hip-roof house on St. Francis Street in St. Augustine was built during the first Spanish colonial period, sometime before 1763. When new, the dwelling probably was a one-story structure that had walls of native limestone, or coquina. It's likely that the second story was added while the British ruled Florida, between 1763 and 1783. When the region was ceded to England, the small stone house belonged to Pedro Fernandez.

Then, as now, its floors were made of tabby — a primitive mortar made of crushed shellstone, lime, sand and water — and its wooden parts were of yellow pine. The second story continued the simple lines of the first, but the front and rear balconies that were added with the new upper level provide shade, protection from showers and cooling breezes that circulate through the house.

During the second period of Spanish rule, from 1783 to 1821, the expanded house belonged to Juan Andreu, the first of several owners of Minorcan descent. The Minorcans had come to America in 1777 to colonize a British community called New Smyrna, and when that plan failed many moved to St. Augustine. The Andreu family owned the coquina house until Florida became a territory of the United States, in 1821. Soon afterward it became the home of Peter and Joseph Manucy. In 1854, the Manucys sold the house to Catalina Llambias, and his family lived there for the next 65 years.

The house was occupied until 1954, when the typically St. Augustine structure was restored to the territorial period of about 1821 to 1845 by members of the St. Augustine Restoration and Preservation Association. Some of its interior walls retain the many layers of paint applied to them over the years, while others reveal the lathing-and-shingling techniques used in the house's construction.

Among noteworthy furnishings are a drop-leaf table-and-chair set that are reproductions of originals made in Minorca for the house, an image of Nuestra Senora de Monto Toro, patroness of Minorca, spirit lamps, rugs and a small table that once belonged to the Llambias family. The upstairs bedrooms are furnished with English, Spanish and early American pieces from that period.

The Fernandez-Llambias House, 33 St. Francis St. in St. Augustine, is open 2 p.m. to 4 p.m. the third Sunday of each month. No admission is charged. For further information, call (904) 824-9823.

NORTHEAST FLORIDA

XIMENEZ-FATIO HOUSE

The house on Aviles Street was built around 1798 for Andres Ximenez, a Spanish merchant who operated a public hall on the ground floor and lived above it with his family.

By the 1820s, the two-story coquina building had been converted into a boarding hotel that was operated by a series of gentlewomen. Margaret Cook, Eliza Whitehurst, Sara Petty Anderson and, finally, Louisa Maria Philipa Fatio ran it.

Many guests were invalids who had come south for the winter to recuperate. It was the earliest and one of the most popular seasonal hotels in St. Augustine. The dining room was open to the public, and was considered to have the best food in town during Louisa Fatio's ownership from 1855 to 1875.

In 1939, the building was purchased by the National Society of Colonial Dames of America in the State of Florida. It at first was valued as an example of late-18th century residential architecture. But the society decided its more interesting period had been the early 19th century. That was when Florida attained territorial status — and, soon after, statehood — and when tourists flocked to the South, particularly to St. Augustine. The house was listed in the National Register of Historic Places in 1973.

It was restored as a 19th century boarding hotel. Among its features are the kitchen that stands separate from the house and has the only original brick baking oven in the city; the Fatio family's horsehair-covered sofa in their private sitting room; and such 19th-century "modernizations" as the addition of Greek Revival architectural detailing.

Charmingly — and authentically — mismatched 19th century chairs appear ready to welcome guests at the long table in the ground-floor dining room. Mosquito netting hangs from the tester of a mahogany high-post bed. English china that belonged to Sarah Anderson is on display. So are chairs and sofas covered with white linen slipcovers, as they were much of the year in St. Augustine more than a century ago. Sheer curtains hang in many windows, and exterior shutters provide shade.

The arms of the U-shaped house wrap around the yard and a broad, two-story porch looks out on it. The courtyard behind the stuccoed house is now washed with sunshine by day, but when the house was a hotel the courtyard was deeply shaded by citrus and other trees. Household tasks were carried out in the courtyard, through which visitors approached the house.

The Ximenez-Fatio House, 20 Aviles St. in St. Augustine, is open from March 1 to Sept. 31. Hours are 11 a.m. to 4 p.m. Thursday through Saturday, 1 a.m. to 4 p.m. Sunday. There is no admission charge. For further information, call (904) 829-3575.

FLORIDA HISTORIC HOMES

DR. PECK HOUSE

Begun around 1710, the gracious Dr. Peck House in St. Augustine was originally owned by the Spanish government and was built as the home of Spaniard Estevan de Pena, the crown's royal treasurer.

Typical of such structures, the house first was one story high and was made of coquina stone with floors of tabby, a mortar made of sand, crushed shells, lime and water. Like many other Spaniards in the remote colonial outpost, de Pena left St. Augustine when the British moved in to occupy it after Spain relinquished Florida in the 1763 Treaty of Paris.

It is likely that the house acquired its glazed windows, fireplaces and chimneys during the 20 years when the British ruled Florida. But even after Spain reclaimed the region in 1783, de Pena did not return to his home.

The already venerable house was sold in 1791 to Francisco Xavier Sanchez, and changed hands several more times before Florida became a U.S. territory in 1821. Sixteen years later, the house became the property of Seth Peck, a physician from Whitesboro, N.Y. He lived in the house and also used it as his clinic.

In 1835, Peck added a wooden second story, as well as wooden floors over the old tabby, and made other improvements. He and his wife, Sarah Lay Peck, furnished the house with elegant 18th century English Chippendale- and Hepplewhite-style pieces that were her dowry, and added a collection of fine oil paintings. The Peck furniture and the oil paintings remain in the house.

The house has three bedrooms on the second floor, as well as the Grand Drawing Room and a sitting room. Downstairs are the old coquina-walled kitchen, which may date to about 1690, a large dining room and Dr. Peck's apothecary and office. Outside, visible from the second-story balcony, is an enclosed garden.

The house remained in the Peck family until 1931, when Dr. Peck's granddaughter, Anna Burt, left the house to the city with the stipulation that it be exhibited as an antebellum home. The city, unable to afford maintenance of the house on the $1,000 left by Miss Burt, awarded custodianship of the house to the Woman's Exchange. The club, which sold and still sells handmade items, agreed to open the house to the public. The group devotes one room to its shop.

The Dr. Peck House is at 143 St. George St. in St. Augustine. Hours are 10 a.m. to 4 p.m. Monday through Saturday; 10 a.m. to 4 p.m. Sunday. An admission is charged. For further information, call (904) 829-5064.

RAINTREE RESTAURANT

When the century-old frame home of Hattie Masters was transformed into the Raintree Restaurant in 1981, its new owners had it stripped down to the bare wood and completely restored before adding a new dining wing.

Patches of surviving tin roof were replaced on the house, which was built between 1879 and 1885. Windows, walls, brackets and other wooden architectural elements were either restored or replaced with duplicates of the cypress originals. The new porch ceilings feature tongue-and-groove construction, just as the old ones did. All four fireplaces are in their original locations, although antique mantels from other old homes were installed on the two first-floor fireplaces.

The house's history stretches back to the days of the second Spanish period in St. Augustine. It stands on land that was given to Gen. Joseph Hernandez, Florida's first territorial delegate to Congress and the man who in 1837 captured Seminole leader Osceola under a flag of truce.

Forty years later, the land was purchased at public auction by Bernard Masters, a 37-year-old Confederate veteran who also was a prominent Minorcan rancher and real estate owner. The land was known as the Masters Tract, and the first house built on it was the Homestead. The Masters raised their five daughters there. They added other buildings on the property, among them the building now known as the Raintree Restaurant and the identical house that once stood beside it.

In 1897, when she married St. Augustine dry-goods merchant A.J. Collins, Hattie Masters became the owner of the house at 102 San Marco Ave. Her sister moved into the matching house when she married, and Masters' daughters raised their children in the two trim Victorian homes. The Raintree house, the only one of the Masters' houses still standing, became a boarding house for a few years at the end of the Second World War and then was converted into the first of three restaurants, the Corner House. The families that operated the first two restaurants in the old house lived on the second floor.

Today's restored Raintree Restaurant closely resembles a Victorian Florida Vernacular house. Its two-story porches are ornamented with turned spindles and lacy brackets, and its crisp clapboards are painted a terra-cotta color.

The Raintree Restaurant is at 102 San Marco Ave. in St. Augustine. It is open daily 11:30 a.m. to 2:30 p.m. for lunch, and 5 p.m. to 9:30 p.m. for dinner. For further information, call (904) 829-5953.

FLORIDA HISTORIC HOMES

CASA DE SOLANA

Completed in 1763 for wealthy native St. Augustinian Don Manuel Solana, the two-and-a-half-story coquina structure in St. Augustine was converted into a bed-and-breakfast hotel in 1982. Its style and materials make it a typical, if grand, St. Augustine building, with its *balcon de la calle,* or street balcony, projecting from its second story and its use of local stone.

Solana, a descendant of the first white settler born in America, chose to stay in St. Augustine after 1763, when Florida was ceded to England by Spain in the Treaty of Paris. After most of the city's Spanish residents fled to Cuba, Solana remained to settle real estate claims. He married in 1777, and had 18 children with his wife, who was 14 when they married. Solana died in 1825, one of St. Augustine's wealthiest citizens.

His house — said to be the seventh-oldest in the city — reflects his prominence as it also reflects the city's architectural heritage. It combines coquina, a locally quarried shell stone, with wood — in this case hand-pegged pine floors and hand-hewn yellow pine joists that run the depth of the structure to support the balconies. Unlike many of St. Augustine's historic homes, which evolved from simple wooden or tabby modules, Solana's 21-room house was a noteworthy residence from the start: It had English-style fireplaces built into the walls rather than the braziers the Spanish settlers were accustomed to placing in the center of the rooms. The floor plan, however, was purely Spanish, with the entrance opening into the gentleman's living room and each room opening into another.

Sturdy beams were left exposed in many rooms, and fine paneling lined some walls. Windows were large, deep-seated and paned with glass in the English fashion. Hearths were made of marble.

Much of the house remains as it was. A porch was enclosed to create a foyer and some downstairs floors are now tiled. The original 19th century paneling remains and the home is furnished with 18th century English antiques.

Casa de Solana is at 21 Aviles St. in St. Augustine. For further information, call (904) 824-3555.

VICTORIAN HOUSE

The cream-colored, blue-trimmed Victorian House in St. Augustine was built in the mid-1880s by Albert Rogero on the site of an earlier Spanish structure.

The Rogero family, descendants of Minorcans who had fled to St. Augustine from New Smyrna a century earlier, lived in the house and rented out some if its rooms until 1904.

It isn't known who owned the two-story frame house in the following 30 or so years. But in the 1940s, the Meyers family bought it and converted it to a private home. The present owner, Daisy Morden, purchased the house in 1983 and opened it as a bed-and-breakfast.

The porch, which extends across the entire facade, is decorated with typically Victorian turned spindles and brackets. The downstairs rooms feature 10-foot-high ceilings, heart-pine floors, and simply crafted heart-pine woodwork.

The rooms are furnished with a mixture of country Victorian antiques, among them a canopy spool cherry bed and several iron and brass beds. The walls are decorated with stenciling, and the rooms feature a collection of hand-hooked rugs, Amish quilts, woven coverlets and early lace.

Additional buildings on the property include a carriage house and a combination kitchen and wash house that now is a potter's shop. The house is on one of St. Augustine's original residential blocks.

Victorian House Bed and Breakfast is at 11 Cadiz St., St. Augustine. For further information, call (904) 824-5414.

CHAPTER IV

CENTRAL FLORIDA

FLORIDA HISTORIC HOMES

Zone III:
CENTRAL FLORIDA

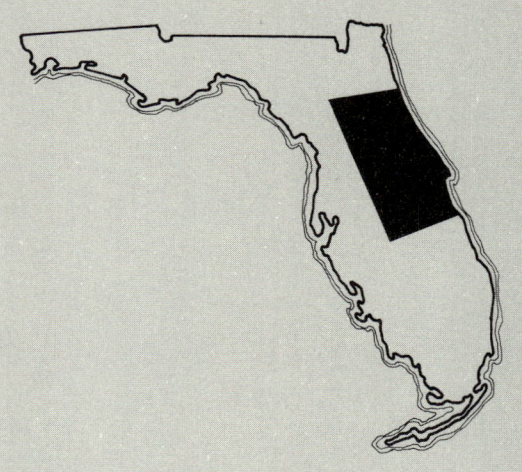

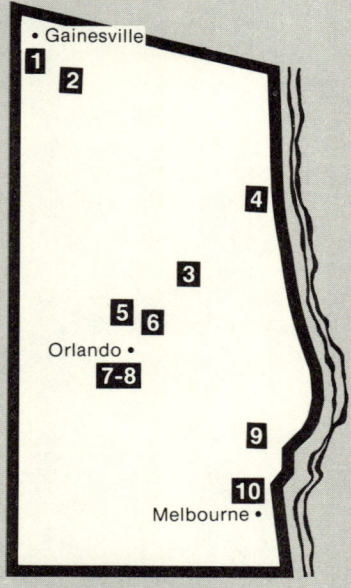

1. Herlong Mansion, Micanopy
2. Marjorie Kinnan Rawlings House, Cross Creek
3. Thursby House, Blue Spring State Park
4. The Casements (John D. Rockefeller House), Ormond Beach
5. Townsend's Plantation, Apopka
6. Bradlee-McIntyre House, Longwood
7. Harry P. Leu House, Orlando
8. Norment-Parry Inn, Orlando
9. E.P. Porcher House, Cocoa
10. Nannie Lee's Strawberry Mansion Restaurant

Steamboats and Citrus Groves

Central Florida includes the areas around Orlando, Daytona Beach, Cocoa and Gainesville. When the Spanish arrived in Florida in the 16th century, much of the zone was inhabited by members of the Timucuan tribe. This tribe became extinct by the 1700s largely because of diseases contracted from whites, warfare with other tribes and the slavery imposed by Europeans.

During the first half of the 19th century, most of Central Florida was part of a vast, relatively undifferentiated tract known bluntly as Mosquito County. But later, Union soldiers returned home from the Civil War with tales of the region's warm, healthful climate and lush landscape.

The area's terrain varies widely, from the low-lying St. Johns River near the coast to the sandy Central Highlands. Although it was settled much later than St. Augustine and the Panhandle, its location between the two coasts and its navigable waterways brought people to Central Florida early on.

One incursion had tragic results. On Dec. 28, 1835, Maj. Francis Dade and 139 soldiers were marching through open pine and palmetto country, near present-day Leesburg, when a band of Seminoles descended on them and killed all but two. The incident led to the last Seminole War, which ended with the near-extinction of the tribe.

The region, however, has long been associated with more pleasant memories. Soon after the Civil War, the Golden Age of Steamships began in Florida. Visitors seeking warm sun and citrus cruised along the natural waterways to such sites as Blue Spring, where the Thursby family established a landing, a home and even a post office.

By the 1880s, when the railroads took the place of the boats and tourism was rapidly increasing, a number of Central Florida cities were founded and prospered. The homes that were built in Mellonville (now Sanford), Orlando, Blue Spring, Micanopy, DeLand and Cocoa reflect the economy and taste of each location. Yet they also show a sensitivity to the climate and dominant architectural styles, such as the high Victorian Queen Anne, Gothic, Classical Revival and simple vernacular Cracker.

FLORIDA HISTORIC HOMES

HERLONG MANSION BED & BREAKFAST

The center section of the massive, three-story Herlong mansion in Micanopy was built in 1875 by R.S. Stoughton. His granddaughter later married V.C. Herlong, a lumberman and citrus grower who had come to Micanopy from South Carolina.

The early house had a kitchen connected to the main wing by a breezeway. Around 1915, Herlong transformed the simple house into an imposing mansion. He added front rooms and another story, incorporating the kitchen and encasing the old frame structure in a brick shell built in a pleasant Classic Revival imitation of the Southern plantation design.

The interior, finished in the Arts and Crafts style of the early 20th century, boasts architectural ornamentation that showcases the hardwood of his trade.

The exterior of the 15-room house is gracious. Its two-story veranda on the facade is supported by enormous Corinthian columns. On the second-level porch, the huge, ornate capitals of the carved-wood columns barely rise above the trim railings.

The view from the veranda is of a garden shaded by oak and pecan trees, a brick front walk to the street and a low brick fence separating the land from historic Cholokka Boulevard, the town's main street.

In 1987, while restoring the mansion, Kim and Simone Evans, owners of the bed-and-breakfast hotel, stripped away layers of wax and varnish from inlaid floors, paneling and trim. They discovered that seven kinds of wood — including maple, walnut, cedar, cypress and mahogany — had been used in the construction and remodeling. About 90 percent of the interior is now tiger oak. The original portion was made of pine. Two of the guest bedrooms, with their fireplaces and pine floors, and two downstairs fireplaces remain from the original house.

The rooms in the bed-and-breakfast contain furnishings in a combination of periods from Victorian to early '30s. Among them are ornately carved, antique Victorian bedsteads and needlepointed, balloon-backed chairs.

Other mansion highlights are its 10 fireplaces, stately floor-to-ceiling dining room windows that allow for three-way cross ventilation, 12-foot ceilings and leaded-glass windows.

Micanopy, a town known for its historic buildings and antique shops, is a 30-minute drive from Silver Springs, Ocala and the horse farms. It is 15 minutes from Gainesville and the University of Florida, and about 30 minutes from Marjorie Kinnan Rawlings' house at Cross Creek.

Room rates vary at the Herlong Mansion, on Cholokka Boulevard in Micanopy. For further information, call (904) 466-3322.

FLORIDA HISTORIC HOMES

RAWLINGS HOUSE

The Rawlings House, a simple Cracker structure, was the full-time home of author Marjorie Kinnan Rawlings from 1928 until 1941. There, often sitting on her porch, at a large table with a base made from a cabbage palm log, she wrote *Cross Creek*, the Pulitzer Prize-winning *The Yearling* and other novels and short stories.

When Rawlings bought the house and 74 acres in 1928 and moved to Florida from the Northeast, it was to devote herself to writing Gothic romances. But her approach changed, with the encouragement of editor Maxwell Perkins. Her writing became based on her backwoods neighbors, local flora and fauna, and her life as a hard-working orange grove owner.

The frame house was built around 1890 with a raised floor and a pitched, sheet metal roof. Its vernacular style is well-adapted to Central Florida's climate. Typical of countless Cracker houses that once dotted the state, it has open porches that admit breezes in the hot summers, and offer shelter from the sun and frequent rainstorms. The many windows in the Rawlings House permit cross-ventilation. The original location of its kitchen (away from the main living and sleeping areas) assured that the heat of the wood-fired kitchen range remained at a distance. The separation of the living and cooking areas not only was practical in a hot climate, but also made sense in a flammable structure.

Even though the Rawlings House was well-designed for a subtropical climate, it had to be heated during Central Florida's occasional cold spells. The author kept warm during the sharp chills by building fires in fireplaces and small stoves, but she also was known to climb into her bed and write by lantern light.

As her writing sold, Rawlings made improvements on her house, among them an indoor bathroom in 1933 and electricity in 1944. And she covered her lamps' bulbs with upturned wooden bowls to create soft, warm, indirect light.

Rawlings' house is furnished comfortably, with several deerhide chairs and the cabbage palm pedestal table. Her hand-carved pine bed once belonged to noted 19th century Florida historian George Fairbanks. To re-create the period when Rawlings lived in the house — when the Floridians around her were neither wealthy snowbirds nor speculators, but people making a barebones living even before the Depression — an outhouse like hers was brought to the site. And to create a sense of how the house looked during Rawlings' long stay, an old typewriter with paper rolled in the carriage sits and waits on the porch.

In 1941, Rawlings married Norton Baskin, a hotelier in St. Augustine, and began dividing her time between the old city and Cross Creek. She died at Crescent Beach in 1953. The author, who made Florida her home and her stories part of history, is buried at Antioch Cemetery in Island Grove. On her tombstone is inscribed: "Marjorie Kinnan Rawlings, 1896-1953 ... Through her writings she endeared herself to the people of the world."

The Marjorie Kinnan Rawlings house in Cross Creek, 21 miles south of Gainesville, is open from 10 to 11:30 a.m. and 1 to 4:30 p.m. Thursday through Monday. Admission is charged. For further information, call (904) 466-3672.

CENTRAL FLORIDA

FLORIDA HISTORIC HOMES

THURSBY HOUSE

The Thursby House in Blue Spring was built by Louis Thursby, a settler who, soon after his arrival in Florida, constructed one of the first steamboat landings and planted one of the first orange groves on the upper St. Johns River.

When the enterprising Thursby settled in 1856 with his family on acreage surrounding Blue Spring and its sandy inlet, he first built a log cabin. But Thursby prospered as steamship travel on the St. Johns increased at the end of the Civil War, bringing tourists and settlers to Florida. He became instrumental in developing Blue Spring into a major stop on the watery route. He encouraged other landowners to bring their crops to his pier for shipment to the North, and eventually connected his landing to nearby Orange City by rail.

Once he was able to afford a finer home, he built the Thursby House, a two-story frame structure, from three kinds of center-cut pine that had been milled in Savannah, Ga., and transported by boat to the site.

The original Thursby house was built in 1872. In 1900, Louis' son added a third story and kitchen wing, which have since been removed. The house has been restored to the way it appeared from 1875 to 1887, the Golden Age on the St. Johns River and the time when Florida was changing from a frontier into a modern state. The Thursby House evokes the era of the steamship. That era ended when trains cut travel time on the St. Johns and also began transporting tourists farther south.

Reminders of that long-gone era at the Thursby House are its cypress water tank, a necessity in an area of sulfurous springs where clean water was a valuable resource, and the cast-iron stoves in each of its rooms. (There was no central fireplace or hearth in the typical raised frame structure, which was highly flammable.) The house stands as it did a century ago, in the heart of a Florida hammock near the river that once was the lifeblood of the region.

The Thursby House is in Blue Spring State Park, 2100 W. French Ave. near Orange City. Guided tours are given at 11 a.m., 1 p.m., 2 p.m., 3 p.m. and 4 p.m. Thursday through Sunday. There is an admission for those over age 6. For further information, call (904) 775-3663.

THE CASEMENTS

This sprawling Ormond Beach mansion is known as "the Rockefeller House," but it was built by the Rev. Harwood Huntington, an Episcopal minister.

The three-story, 80-room home was constructed in the early 1900s in a pleasant, shingled style that was popular at the time. It was designed so that most of its casement windows overlooked either the Halifax River or the Atlantic Ocean.

In 1918, however, the Huntingtons tired of Florida and moved to California. They sold their rambling mansion to Standard Oil founder John D. Rockefeller, who was ailing and had chosen Ormond Beach as a place to live. The oil magnate considered this place the healthiest spot on earth. He had wintered earlier at the nearby Hotel Ormond, and found the climate so fine that he bought the Huntington house and set about making improvements.

Rockefeller had the rooms extended, the wide galleries enclosed and a handsome wrought-iron fence built. He brought his five sons to The Casements, and used it as his winter home until he died there in 1937, at age 98.

In 1941, the historic property became a women's junior college, and a concrete-block dormitory was added. A decade later, it became a retirement center. In the '60s, the house was slated for demolition to make way for a condominium. In the early 1970s, however, the decaying, vandalized house was listed on the National Register of Historic Places and bought by the city of Ormond Beach, which converted it to a community center that offers classes and art exhibits.

Its present austere condition

hardly reflects the house's earlier grandeur. When it belonged to Rockefeller, the house featured an octagonal living room and a three-story entrance decorated with a Louis Comfort Tiffany stained-glass skylight. Velvet draperies hung in the casement windows, and gardens of sea grapes, laurel hedges, hibiscus, oleander and roses swept from the house to water's edge. Goldfish swam in pools in the gardens, where paths were arranged in geometric patterns that followed the hedges and crisscrossed beds of flowers.

The Casements, at 25 Riverside Drive in Ormond Beach, is open from 9 a.m. to 9 p.m. Monday through Thursday, 9 a.m. to 5 p.m. Friday and 9 a.m. to noon on Saturday. Free tours are conducted 10 a.m. to 3 p.m. Monday through Friday, 10 a.m. to noon Saturday. For further information, call (904) 673-4701.

FLORIDA HISTORIC HOMES

BRADLEE-MCINTYRE HOUSE

This turreted Victorian mansion, the last of the elegant winter "cottages" once common in the Altamonte Springs area, was built in 1885 for the Nathan Bradlee family of Boston.

When it was new, the house stood on what is now the busy intersection of Maitland Avenue and State Road 436 in Altamonte Springs. (It was moved in the early 1970s.)

But when it was new, the large 15-room, Queen Anne-style home was in the country, far from an Orlando that then had sandy roads and a small population. At that time, Altamonte Springs and the areas around it were resort centers for Northerners drawn by Central Florida's mild winters. Many of them stayed at the famous Altamonte Springs Hotel.

Over the years, the rambling three-story frame house acquired an unlikely legend. Although U.S. President and Civil War general Ulysses S. Grant died the year it was built, a persistent rumor had it that he visited or slept in this house. The truth was that after the general's death, his son and/or his wife spent time vacationing at the house.

It changed hands several times between 1899 and 1904, when the mansion became the property of S. Maxwell McIntyre. Earlier, he had bought most of the town of Altamonte Springs from the Altamonte Land, Hotel & Navigation Co. The McIntyres occupied the house until 1946.

But by the 1970s, the mansion had fallen on hard times and was threatened with demolition. Deserted and vandalized, it was placed on the National Register of Historic Places and moved to Longwood by the Central Florida

Society for Historic Preservation.

It has been substantially restored to its earlier grandeur, both inside and out. Among its notable features are the octagonal turret that is clad with a decorative pattern made of shingles of varying shapes; the ornate "gingerbread" woodwork that ornaments the deep gables; and the broad, first-story veranda.

The house has been furnished in styles of the late Victorian period. Living room furnishings include a turn-of-the-century Steinway piano, a rosewood Empire sofa and matching gooseneck rocker, a small Victorian love seat and a large pier mirror. The living room and dining room are papered in soft green-and-white patterned paper.

Bedroom furnishings include a carved Victorian bed and a Jenny Lind spool bed that were in the house when the McIntyres lived there.

The Bradlee-McIntyre House is at 150 W. Warren St. in Longwood. Hours are 11 a.m. to 4 p.m., second and fourth Wednesdays. An admission is charged. For further information, call (407) 332-6920.

CENTRAL FLORIDA

TOWNSEND'S PLANTATION

Now a restaurant, but once a residence, this Apopka house continues to evoke 19th century Florida. The turreted house was built in 1903 by the Eldredge family, whose descendants still live in the Central Florida community. In the 1920s, the eight-room frame structure became the home and clinic of Dr. T.E. McBride, one of Apopka's first physicians. After his death in 1978, it sat empty for several years.

Finally, in 1985, the 4,000-square-foot, Queen Anne house was divided into four sections and moved to its present site off U.S. Highway 441 at Martin's Pond. It was enlarged and transformed into a restaurant with a Victorian atmosphere. Its latest owners removed the termite-damaged kitchen and a bathroom, and added about 10,000 square feet to the elegant building, but retained its highly ornamental character. There now is dining in all rooms of the three-story house.

The high-ceilinged rooms are furnished with antiques and are papered with Victorian-style patterns that are in keeping with its period of ornate design. Every room has a different theme: One is done as a children's rumpus room, complete with antique toys and paintings of children; another is a game room that features a deep-brown-and-black color scheme, thick brocades on chair seats, and old golf clubs and hunting trophies.

Two of the rooms have been dedicated to the McBrides, and among the objects displayed in the rooms are 1940s-vintage photographs of Mrs. McBride in some of the airplanes she flew.

The restaurant's owners spent about a year collecting period furnishings. Many of its oak tables and chairs came from the old Ormond Beach Hotel, long a coastal landmark. The carpet in the main dining room has a Victorian pattern, and adds to the overall re-creation of the 19th century in Florida.

The house features floors and woodwork in Florida heart pine, as well as doors, casings and a staircase that are in their elaborate, original state. The fireplace tiles are in greens and aquamarines. A broad porch wraps around the facade on the first floor, raised above ground level; dormers and picturesque chimneys project from the steep roof in a complex jumble of asymmetrical massing that is typical of the Queen Anne style.

Today, the greatly expanded old Eldredge-McBride House is painted a crisp white with dark green trim, and sits comfortably on an open site in Apopka.

Townsend's Plantation is at 604 E. Main St. in Apopka, at the intersection of U.S. Highway 441 and State Road 436. High tea is served from 3 p.m. to 4 p.m. Monday through Saturday, and dinner from 5 p.m. to 11 p.m. Monday through Saturday. For further information, call (407) 880-1313.

FLORIDA HISTORIC HOMES

HARRY P. LEU HOUSE

When the first section of the Harry P. Leu House was built, sometime between 1870 and 1901, the four-room farmhouse stood in the country. The house consisted of a living room downstairs and three bedrooms above it. It was built for John Mizell, son of one of Orange County's founders, and his bride. Over the years, various owners added and subtracted rooms from the once-simple farmhouse, leaving it finally with 10 graciously furnished rooms.

The trim house, now not far from booming downtown Orlando, stands in a 56-acre garden with charming wooden gazebos and thousands of exotic flowers and plants, among them forests of camellias and avenues of giant camphors. This land is what remains of the 103 acres claimed on the shores of Lake Rowena by Angeline May Mizell while her husband was fighting for the Confederacy during the Civil War.

The first structure on the site was the family's log cabin, which stood near the present house. The nearby Mizell family graveyard may still be visited.

In the early years of the century, while the Leu farmhouse was owned by a wealthy New Yorker who came to Florida to plant citrus and play polo, it gained a kitchen, dining room, more upstairs bedrooms and wraparound porches. Between 1906 and 1928, it was the home of a wealthy Birmingham industrialist who wintered there with his large family and staff. In 1936, it became the property of Leu, a prosperous businessman and Orlando native who loved trees and flowers. He and his wife transformed the estate into a tropical paradise, and in 1961 donated the greatly expanded farmhouse to the city of Orlando.

The restored interior of the house features the sort of period furnishings and decor a successful citrus grower might have had between the 1870s and the early 1900s. Pieces on display include an ornate, carved bed; Gov. Napoleon Bonaparte Broward's mahogany library table; and a round oak table and server from the Joseph A. Bumby home in Orlando.

The Harry P. Leu House, 1730 N. Forest Ave., Orlando, is open from 9 a.m. to 5 p.m. daily except Christmas, and tours of the house are conducted every half hour. An admission is charged. For further information, call (407) 849-2620.

CENTRAL FLORIDA

NORMENT-PARRY INN

The downtown Orlando Norment-Parry Inn was built for Judge Richard B. Norment of Baltimore and his wife, Margaret Parry, between 1883 and 1885 as their permanent home. It was built at a time when Orlando was a small community with sandy roads and a largely agrarian economy. The oldest documented house extant in Orlando, this two-story, Victorian structure is now a bed-and-breakfast hotel.

A wide, open porch projects from its frame facade, and the screened porch on the east side on the ground floor, like the tall, narrow windows throughout, offer light and cross-ventilation. Among its original features are the ornate, typically Victorian wooden scrollwork on the front-porch columns and interior woodwork.

The house was built of Florida hardwood. The L-shaped structure was enlarged in the 1920s, when gas lighting was installed. A summer kitchen also was added. During the 19th and early 20th centuries, the house was the setting for key events in the lives of a number of prominent Orlandoans: In 1893, Margaret Thornton was born there, and the next year Harry Bumby and Ella West were married in the parlor.

More recently, the clapboard house on Lake Lucerne, in Orlando's Lake Cherokee Historic District, has served as a rooming house and an alcohol-rehabilitation center. In 1986, it was renovated and refurbished in a fanciful Victorian style to become a bed-and-breakfast inn. Its seven guest suites, parlor and other rooms are furnished with American and English antiques.

The Norment-Parry Inn is at 211 N. Lucerne Circle E. in Orlando. Room rates vary. For further information, call (407) 648-5188.

FLORIDA HISTORIC HOMES

E.P. PORCHER HOUSE

The elegant, coquina-stone house in Cocoa was built around 1915 for citrus grower E.P. Porcher and his wife, Byrnina Peck. The house is on the National Register of Historic Places, and the stone used to build it was quarried locally.

Porcher, co-founder of the Florida Citrus Commission, and an innovator, believed that the fruit he grew in his Deerfield Citrus Groves would bring a higher price at market if it were washed, stamped and attractively packaged. So he invented the first fruit-washing machine, a dolly for lifting packed fruit for storage and shipment, and the fruit stamp for labeling his produce.

Several historical styles are combined in this house that citrus built, a symmetrical, three-story stone structure. The two-story, semicircular porch at the entrance is reminiscent of a Renaissance or Classical temple, and the pediment of the dormer directly over the entrance porch evokes images of Greek architecture. The house itself is more than 5,000 square feet in size, and is in a pleasant Federal style.

Mrs. Porcher's interest in bridge shows in the club, spade, diamond and heart-shaped designs carved in the coquina stone on the house's back porch.

Inside, the house is impressive. A central staircase with squared spindles on its balustrade leads from the first floor to the second. There are five rooms on the first floor, along with a foyer, gallery and kitchen. The downstairs ceilings are 14 feet high. There are nine rooms on the second floor, where ceilings are 12 feet high. When the house was used by the Porcher family, the third floor contained bedrooms.

When the coquina-stone mansion on the Indian River was new, a warehouse and packing plant stood nearby. The packing-and-storage house was known in Cocoa as the "fruit laundry." Later, it was torn down to allow for widening of the riverfront property. The house currently is unfurnished.

The E.P. Porcher House, 434 Delannoy Ave. in Cocoa, is open 8 a.m. to 5 p.m. weekdays, 10 a.m. to 2 p.m. Saturday and by appointment. For further information, call (407) 639-7564.

CENTRAL FLORIDA

NANNIE LEE'S STRAWBERRY MANSION

When the gingerbread-clad, three-story house was new, around 1905, it was the winter home of Nannie McBride Lee and her husband, John B. Lee. Today, it is a restaurant with a turn-of-the-century atmosphere, thanks to the soundness of its tin-roofed, frame structure, and to its elaborate design.

The restaurant is named for its original owner, who was born in Clark County, Ill., in 1847 and lived in Albion, N.Y., until her marriage to businessman John Lee in 1894. The couple arrived in quiet Melbourne in 1905 and built their ornate, cold-weather getaway. Not long after the house was completed, however, the couple started living in it year-round.

Nannie Lee quickly became active in the Melbourne community, and the house became the center for numerous social, religious and civic activities — among them Nannie's memorable ice-cream socials.

In its early years, the sturdy house also occasionally served as a hurricane shelter. Its particularly fine oak staircase, bay window and gingerbread trim were crafted by the Lees' neighbor to the west, a boat builder and carpenter named Claude Beaujean. His family operated the Atlantic Ferry service, which crossed the Indian River five times each day before a bridge linked the city to the nearby beaches.

When Nannie Lee died in 1929, the house became the property of her adopted daughter, Lily Tidwell.

Lily and her husband, then the owner of Melbourne's only gas station, raised their children in the house and lived there until Lily's death. Her heirs sold the property.

It was first rented and then left empty until its current owners bought it in 1975. They spent six years restoring the dilapidated mansion, removing layers of old paint from handsome oak beams, Ionic columns and an ornate fireplace. They landscaped its yard with crotons, azaleas and palms, and shopped at garage sales, flea markets and antique shops to find the vintage furnishings that now grace its dining rooms.

Nannie Lee's Strawberry Mansion, 1218 E. New Haven Ave. in Melbourne, is open 4:30 to 9 p.m. weekdays, 4:30 to 10 p.m. weekends. For further information, call (407) 724-8627.

CHAPTER V

SOUTHWEST FLORIDA

FLORIDA HISTORIC HOMES

Zone IV: SOUTHWEST FLORIDA

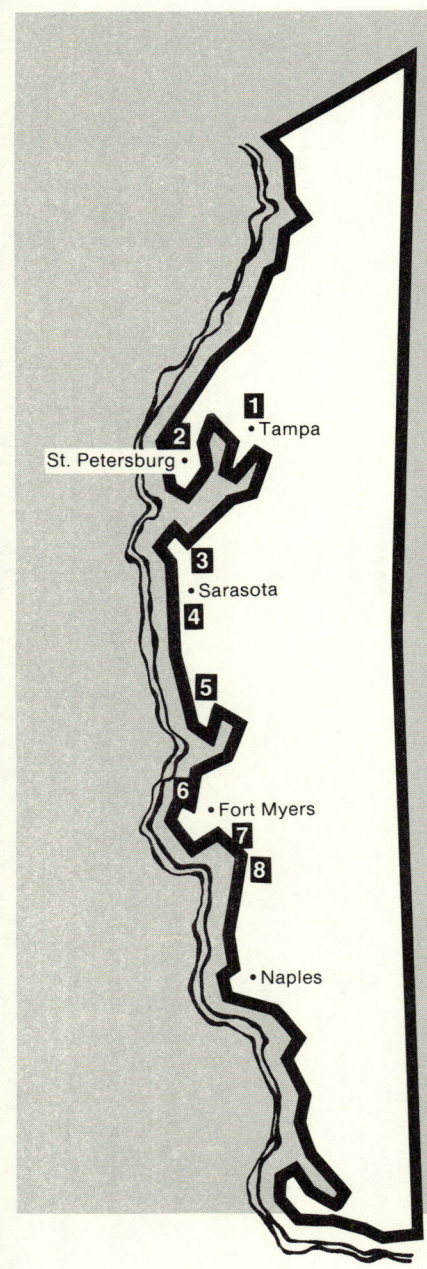

1. Cigar Makers' Houses, Tampa
2. Bayboro House, St. Petersburg
3. Gamble Plantation, Ellenton
4. Ca'd'Zan, Sarasota
5. Banyan House, Venice
6. Cabbage Key Inn and Restaurant, Cabbage Key
7. Edison Winter Home, Fort Myers
8. Koreshan Settlement, Estero

SOUTHWEST FLORIDA

Sun and Sand

The earliest recorded European visit to the Tampa area was in 1528, when Panfilo de Narvaez passed through it on his way north. He was exploring the interior of the New World on the first such expedition. Eleven years later, Hernando de Soto arrived, and promptly conquered an Indian village in order to formally declare Spanish supremacy.

For the next three centuries, there was little development in the region the early Spanish visitors named Bahia de Espiritu Santo. In 1823, soon after Florida became a territory of the young United States, Fort Brooke was constructed of logs. Eight years later, a post office called Tampa Bay opened in the area, and in 1834, the settlement's official name became Tampa, an Indian name meaning "split wood for quick fires." The new fort played an important role in the last of the Seminole Wars — 1835 to 1842 — yet Tampa itself remained a small town and the region around it virtually a wilderness.

During the Civil War, Tampa saw only minor military action. After the Confederacy fell, its population dwindled even further. And when a railroad was built between the east and west coasts, bypassing Tampa, and yellow fever swept the community, the already small population declined still further.

All that changed in 1884, when Henry Plant pushed his railroad through to Tampa, then a town of just a few hundred people. Next, he extended the road 9 miles southwest to Port Tampa, where he built a causeway and piers to deep water to facilitate shipping. As in other parts of Florida where the arrival of the railroad created incredibly rapid development, Tampa seemed to change overnight.

In 1890, the year before Plant built his fabulous, Moorish-style Tampa Bay Hotel, Tampa's population was 5,000. A decade later, with the success of the cigar industry in Ybor City and the discovery of phosphate fields nearby, the population had tripled. Some 30,000 troops were stationed in Tampa during the Spanish-American War, and Col. Theodore Roosevelt trained his Rough Riders on the grounds of the famous hotel, which is now home of the University of Tampa.

As Tampa developed into an industrial center, the nearby areas also saw rapid growth. Sarasota, to the south, had been settled in the 1840s by William Whittaker, a homesteader from Tallahassee who built a log home and planted the area's first orange grove with seeds brought from Cuba.

Later, Hamilton Disston bought 4 million acres in the area and, in 1883, persuaded 60 Scottish families to settle on the land. Three years later, the son of a Scottish settler built a golf course in Sarasota and that, along with fishing and hunting, helped attract vacationers. A pioneer railroad ran to Sarasota in 1892, yet until 1899 the community had only 20 houses and no sidewalks.

It took the arrival of the Seaboard Air Line Railroad in 1902 to transform Sarasota. In 1911, Chicago society leader Mrs. Potter Palmer purchased a 13-acre estate and bought land, and that same year the Ringling Brothers first came to town. Sixteen years later, John Ringling made the once-quiet town the winter home of his circus, the "greatest show on earth," and built his home, the magnificent Ca'd'Zan.

The development of Fort Myers, still farther to the south, was more gradual. Settled near a fort built in 1839 and enlarged in 1850, the area was a thriving agricultural center after the Civil War. Among its crops were mangoes, avocados, papayas, guavas and citrus. Fort Myers also was known for its commercial fishing. Inventor Thomas Alva Edison built a house in the town in 1886, hoping to perfect a bamboo-filament light bulb while working in his winter laboratory and using plants that grew wild on his property. Edison's friends and sponsors, Henry Ford and Harvey Firestone, built winter homes near the inventor's in Fort Myers.

Another railroad, the short-lived Orange Belt, running from Apopka in 1883, brought life to St. Petersburg, a scruffy village barely inhabited by 30 people, including children. Peter Demens, the Americanized name of the immigrant whose dream built the railroad, named the town for his beloved Russian city.

By the early 1900s St. Petersburg was on its way with the arrival of people such as Charles A. Harvey and his plans to build a St. Petersburg harbor.

The stories of the main cities on Florida's west coast are very different from one another, yet all depended for their development on transportation — the train, primarily — and on tourism. As in other parts of Florida, once people came and saw, they came back and stayed.

CIGAR WORKERS' HOUSES

Three frame cottages, now part of the Ybor City State Museum, are typical of those that once were common in the east Tampa community. Moved from their original sites and restored to their appearance in the heyday of cigar-making, from 1895 to 1920, they are houses once occupied by cigar factory workers and their families.

The hand-rolling of cigars became an important industry in Tampa when Don Vicente Martinez Ybor opened his factory in 1886 in the sparsely populated, palmetto-covered frontier. He, like other cigar manufacturers, moved from Key West to avoid employees' demands for higher wages and better working conditions. At one time, the Ybor factory was the largest cigar-producing factory in the world, and employed a fifth of Ybor City's cigar-makers.

The community that sprang up around the factories included Cubans, Germans, Spaniards, Italians and Jews. They established their own newspapers, restaurants, social clubs, mutual-aid societies and hospitals. In addition, the residents continued the simple, practical style of residential architecture that had characterized the Key West cigar-makers' houses.

The houses were built on a long, narrow Spanish-style floor plan that has rooms lined one behind the other opening off a long hallway along one side. Often referred to as *conones* — cannons, or shotgun houses — it was said that a shotgun could be fired from the front door to the back without hitting a wall. Two cottages display exhibits of Ybor City's cigar-making history, but one restored cottage serves as a house museum and is furnished in a simple style typical of the period and social class.

The single-story cigar workers' houses were built in a balloon-type of construction from Florida pine, with hand-split cedar or cypress shakes and pine-plank floors. They had no heat, electricity or running water, and protection from storms and insects was provided by inside shutters and, in the hot seasons, by cheesecloth screening. The earliest houses had cypress or cedar shingles, but after the 1908 fire that destroyed whole blocks of Ybor City, roofs were covered with tin.

The Cigar Workers' Houses are at the Ybor City State Museum, 1818 Ninth Ave., Tampa. They are open from 9 a.m. to noon and 1 p.m. to 5 p.m. Thursdays through Mondays. An admission is charged. For further information, call (813) 247-6323.

FLORIDA HISTORIC HOMES

BAYBORO HOUSE

The two-story St. Petersburg house was built about 1903 by Charles A. Harvey. He was a Jessup, Ga., real estate developer with plans to build a St. Petersburg harbor.

Harvey began the Bayboro Investment Co. and developed some of his St. Petersburg holdings as a residential area. But he died in 1914, before he was able to fulfill his dream of building Bayboro Harbor.

Nonetheless, he was able to complete his own modified Queen Anne-style house on the choicest lot overlooking Tampa Bay, where it still stands. Harvey's house is now a bed-and-breakfast inn.

The 19-room frame-and-shingle house features a wide porch that wraps around the front and side on the first story, a many-gabled roof, an asymmetrical arrangement of large windows in front, and bay windows on both sides of the upper story. The upper portion of the front facade is clad in shingles.

The house has 10-foot ceilings with heart pine beams, 12-inch-high baseboards and woodwork of heart pine crafted in a variety of styles popular at the time. Among its features are the door and window frames that are ornamented with incised designs, and the classical columns that flank the wide doorway between the living room and the dining room.

The house remained in the Harvey family for some years, then changed hands three times, and was purchased in the early 1970s by Gordon and Antonia Powers. They turned it into an inn with three guest suites. They furnished the inn with a fanciful combination of Empire and various Victorian styles, re-creating the mood of the era when the Harvey house was new. Items of interest include an Ampico player piano, a pump organ, marble-topped tables, grandfather clocks and a velvet fainting couch.

Bayboro House is at 1719 Beach Drive, S.E., St. Petersburg. For further information, call (813) 823-4955.

BANYAN HOUSE

This Mediterranean-style house — now a bed-and-breakfast inn — was built in 1926, during the height of Florida's great land boom. It was built for Robert Marvin and his wife. He was an executive with the Brotherhood of Locomotive Engineers, the developers of the planned city of Venice, Fla. When the land boom bottomed out in 1929, the city went bankrupt and became a ghost town. The house, like the rest of the city, was abandoned.

The cream-colored stucco house, with its red barrel tiles and a latticed front door, was designed for luxurious living. It had 10 rooms, pecky cypress ceilings and a carriage house.

But for several years — until Virginia Wilson bought it for back taxes — its inhabitants were hobos. They would camp out on the Italian tiled floors and cook over an open fire in a sculptured fireplace that also had been imported from Italy. During Wilson's ownership, from 1932 to 1962, the house was a nursery school, a guest house and a tearoom, as well as the offices of the city's first taxi service. During the Second World War, the Banyan House became an unofficial headquarters for the USO.

The next owner, Margaret Thomas, wrote books on sharks' teeth and displayed her fossils in the house. It's said that she tossed some of her sharks' teeth rejects into the pool as she worked on her books; the pool did cave in while she lived at the Banyan House. The house got its name in the 1930s, when it was a rooming house, from the gigantic East India tree on the property.

The elegant house was used as a hurricane shelter during the 1930s and 1940s. But in 1979, it was converted into a bed-and-breakfast inn and has been renovated to reflect the city's unusual history and the period when the house was new. The guest rooms in the main house and the carriage house have such names as Palm Room and Palmetto Room, and the swimming pool and hot tub are set in the garden beneath the old banyan tree.

The Banyan House is at 519 S. Harbor Drive in Venice. Rates at the bed-and-breakfast inn vary seasonally. For further information, call (813) 484-1385.

FLORIDA HISTORIC HOMES

GAMBLE PLANTATION

The Gamble Plantation in Ellenton is the only antebellum mansion on Florida's west coast that is still standing. It has survived Indian uprisings, Civil War incursions and natural disasters. The home also is of historic interest because it served, in May 1865, as the hiding place for Judah P. Benjamin, the only Confederate cabinet member to elude capture as the South was falling to the North.

The elegant residence, begun in 1843 and completed in 1850, was built by Maj. Robert Gamble. He was a veteran of the Seminole Wars who had moved from Tallahassee in 1842 to establish an immense sugar-cane plantation.

The Greek Revival structure has walls that are 2 feet thick for insulation. They are made of tabby bricks — tabby is a primitive form of concrete that here is a mixture of lime, crushed oyster shells and perhaps sugar-cane juice — then plastered with more tabby.

The residence is 43 feet wide and 93 feet long, and its 18 25-foot-high columns were, at the time of its construction, considered symbols of sophistication. They are made of wedge-shaped tabby bricks and are nearly 18 inches in diameter. The

columns support verandas on three sides and both levels, in typical Southern mansion style. Those large porches provide a place to sit, and open the home to cool breezes while sheltering it from sunshine and showers.

The mansion's original grounds were vast: Gamble owned a 3,500-acre site, 1,500 of which were cleared and cultivated. In 1855, he had 151 slaves working on the plantation.

Today the restored Gamble mansion looks much as it did when it was new. Inside, it has period furnishings that evoke the spirit of the vanished era. A small sugar-cane field on its grounds represents the hundreds of acres once farmed.

The Gamble Plantation, 3708 Patten Ave., off U.S. Highway 301 at Ellenton, near Bradenton, is open from 9 a.m. until 4 p.m. daily except Tuesday and Wednesday. Tours begin each hour from 9 a.m. An admission is charged for those over 6. For further information, call (813) 722-1017.

FLORIDA HISTORIC HOMES

SOUTHWEST FLORIDA

CA'D'ZAN

The residence of John and Mable Ringling in Sarasota is one of Florida's grandest houses. Completed in 1926 at a cost of about $1.5 million, the structure combined architectural elements drawn from two of Mrs. Ringling's favorites — the facade of the Doge's Palace in Venice and the tower of the old Madison Square Garden in New York, where her husband's circus regularly appeared.

Designed by New York architect Dwight James Baum, the home is made of stucco and terra-cotta tiles in a variety of colors — soft red, yellow, blue, green and ivory. The roof of the two-and-a-half-story structure is covered with thousands of old red barrel tiles bought from Barcelona by Mrs. Ringling, who was involved in the design and construction of the house and gardens.

The mansion's windows are set with handmade Venetian tinted glass. Such elements as columns, doorways, balustrades, tiles and arched windows also were imported from Italy and other countries. The look that the Ringlings and their designer sought was a fanciful Venetian Renaissance style, and their efforts extended to the house's interior. The house is centered by a vast roofed court that served as the main living room, around which 30 bedrooms and 14 baths are located. Service areas such as kitchens and pantries, as well as servants' quarters, are in a wing to the south.

Many of the furnishings at Ca'd'Zan — which in a Venetian dialect means "house of John" — were acquired from the homes of Vincent Astor and Jay Gould. They, in keeping with Ca'd'zan's eclecticism, show the influence of such varied styles as the Italian and French Renaissance and French Baroque. Among the noteworthy furnishings are the $50,000 Aeolian Organ, the Steinway grand piano in its ornamented rosewood case and 17th century Flemish and English tapestries. To add to the house's appeal, the ceilings of its ballroom and game room were painted by Willy Pogany, set designer for the Ziegfeld Follies, and show the Ringlings in fancy-dress costume.

Ca'd'Zan, on U.S. Highway 41 in Sarasota, is open from 10 a.m. to 6 p.m. Friday through Wednesday, 10 a.m. to 10 p.m. Thursday. An admission is charged. For further information, call (813) 355-5101.

FLORIDA HISTORIC HOMES

CABBAGE KEY INN AND RESTAURANT

The pleasant, one-story frame house was completed in 1938 as a winter home for Alan Rinehart. He was the son of American mystery writer Mary Roberts Rinehart, author of *The Circular Staircase* and other well-known damsel-in-distress suspense novels.

The reclusive author Rinehart wrote some of her stories at the Cabbage Key house, as well as at her own home, one of the original beach cottages on nearby Useppa Island. She was very much involved in the design and construction of her son's house.

Alan Rinehart and his wife, Grace, had bought Cabbage Key Island, a tiny island near Fort Myers, in 1929 for $2,500. By the time the house was built, they had spent another $125,000 for the features that may be seen today at the small resort.

The house sits 38 feet above sea level on Cabbage Key. It was constructed on a shell mound built up over the centuries by the Calusa Indians, whose now-extinct civilization dates to about 3,500 B.C.

The house is painted white with green trim, and is surrounded by a screened porch. Inside, the small inn and restaurant are cooled not by air conditioning but by the breezes provided by Bahama fans.

The nature trail on the grounds of the inn, which today includes three guest cottages, winds through a subtropical garden of fan palms, royal poincianas and sabal — or cabbage — palms.

The Alan and Grace Rinehart residence first opened as a hotel in 1942. Among its attractions are its unusual elevation, its Florida Vernacular architectural style and its access to fishing and boating.

Also appealing is its peculiar style of papering its restaurant walls with dollar bills autographed by guests, among them rock musicians Neil Young and Jimmy Buffett. According to Cabbage Key legend, the practice began years ago when a pessimistic patron tacked a dollar on the wall with his name on it. That way, or so the story goes, even if he lost everything, he could still come back to the pleasant island for a drink.

Cabbage Key Inn and Restaurant, on Milemarker 60 in Southwest Florida's barrier islands, may be reached only by boat. Non-boaters may be picked up by reservation on Pine Island at Pineland Marina in Pineland. For further information, call (813) 283-2278.

SOUTHWEST FLORIDA

EDISON WINTER HOME

When inventor Thomas Alva Edison decided to build a winter home for himself and his bride, Mina Miller, on a 14-acre site in Fort Myers, he displayed practicality as well as innovation.

His two-story frame structure on the Caloosahatchee River is typically Victorian in its stick-style — or "gingerbread" — ornamentation and expansive, rambling plan. But it is also well-suited to its subtropical setting, with a broad, shady porch on the ground level, French doors and a tiled colonnade between the main and guest houses.

Shutters on the casement windows offer protection from storms, and fireplaces were built in many rooms to provide warmth from occasional cold spells. The swimming pool was reinforced with bamboo instead of steel, and is filled by an artesian well 1,100 feet deep.

Like many other frame houses in Florida, the trim, New England-style structure is well-adapted to its climate. But, surprisingly, it was not built here. Edison's houses — the main one and the breezeway-connected guest residence — are among the first prefabricated buildings in the country. Edison himself drew the plans. In 1885, the houses were built in sections in Fairfield, Maine. Those sections were shipped to Fort Myers, then largely a wilderness, in four sailing ships and were assembled in 1886. Soon afterward, the couple began wintering in the house.

It is still furnished as it was during their stays, complete with the wicker porch furniture, Edison-designed brass lamps and carbon-filament light bulbs, laboratory, office and car collection.

Edison chose Fort Myers partly

because he wanted to experiment with a bamboo-filament light bulb, and he used the plants that grow plentifully on the property. His laboratory, like the house and garage, has been preserved as he left it. In the lab, visitors may see the inventor's equipment for producing synthetic rubber. In addition, more than 200 Edison phonographs and other Edison memorabilia are on view in the museum.

Edison's tropical botanical garden, where he planted more than a thousand varieties of plants imported from all over the world for experimental purposes, thrives on the grounds. Most noteworthy is the banyan tree: It was 2 inches in diameter in 1925, when Edison's friend and Fort Myers neighbor Harvey Firestone brought it to him from India. The remarkable plant now measures more than 400 feet around its trunks.

The Edison Winter Home, at 2350 McGregor Blvd. in Fort Myers, is open 9 a.m. to 4 p.m. Monday through Saturday, 12:30 to 4 p.m. Sunday. There is an admission for those 6 and older. For further information, call (813) 334-3614.

FLORIDA HISTORIC HOMES

KORESHAN SETTLEMENT

The high-ceilinged, pitched-roofed buildings of the Koreshan Settlement, on the banks of the Estero River near Fort Myers, reflect the idealism of its builders as well as a practical approach to the west coast's subtropical climate.

Constructed during the late 19th and early 20th centuries, the simple frame structures served as living, dining, recreation and working quarters for followers of Cyrus Reed Teed, a religious visionary.

Teed had led his disciples from Chicago to the remote Florida wilderness, establishing a settlement that he named Estero and hoped would grow into a great "New Jerusalem" under his leadership. Teed called himself "Koresh," and his religion "Koreshanity."

Central to his Koreshanity is the belief that the universe is a hollow sphere with the sun in the center and with life existing on the inside.

Teed instituted among his followers a way of life that included celibacy, as well as communal living and ownership of all property. Teed, however, died in 1908 and his community declined, nevertheless leaving evidence of a great deal of creative energy.

Besides the planetary court (home of the all-female Koreshan ruling council), the recreation or art hall, a dining hall and separate living quarters for men and women, there was a bakery, a general store, a shipbuilding shop, a machine shop and agricultural buildings. Among the enterprises that supported the community were the making and selling of baked goods, including a bread made from their special recipe.

The gardens included such tropical plants as agaves, bromeliads, royal palms, sausage trees, avocados, mangos and sapotes.

Of the original buildings, only six remain. Three — the planetary court, the art hall and an area of the bakery — are open for public tour. The oldest building, Teed's home, which was built around 1896, no longer stands.

The art hall and planetary court were built around 1905. The art hall, used then for band concerts, plays and meetings, is a single-story structure of Florida pine with a cypress shake shingle roof and a porch that wraps around the building.

The planetary court, also constructed of pine with cypress shingle roof, consists of two stories with porches on both levels, four bedrooms upstairs, and three bedrooms and a meeting room downstairs.

Furnishings in the two buildings, all brought from the North by the Koreshans, are of the late 19th century Victorian style. Visitors find the furnishings surprisingly elegant considering the then-remote Florida frontier location.

In 1961, the four surviving members decided to deed 305 acres of the Koreshan property to the state as a historical site.

The organization exists today as the World College of Life, a historical organization with headquarters across the highway from the park.

The Koreshan Community at the Koreshan State Park is open from 9 a.m. to 4 p.m. every day. Guided tours of the buildings are conducted at 10:30 a.m. and 2:30 p.m. from mid-December to mid-March and at 1 p.m. during the off season. Estero is 25 miles south of Fort Myers on U.S. Highway 41. There is an admission to the park for visitors over age 6. For further information, call (813) 992-0311.

CHAPTER VI

SOUTH FLORIDA

FLORIDA HISTORIC HOMES

Zone V:
SOUTH FLORIDA

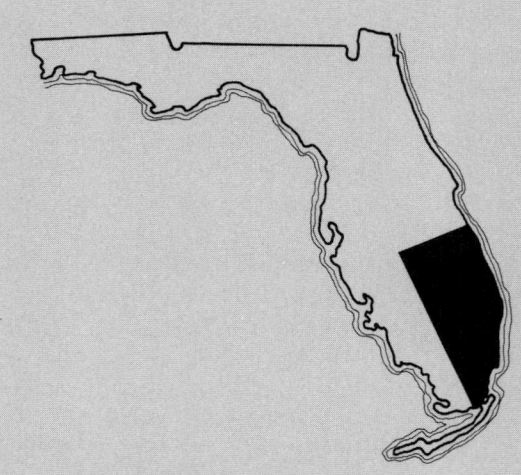

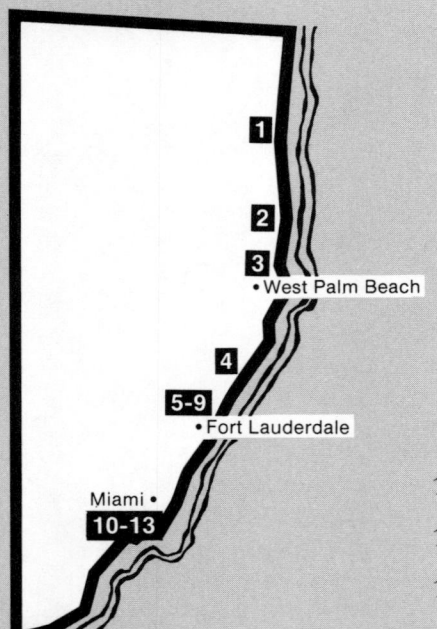

1. Gilbert's Bar House of Refuge, Hutchinson Island
2. Dubois Home, Jupiter Inlet
3. Whitehall (Henry Morrison Flagler Museum), Palm Beach
4. La Vieille Maison, Boca Raton
5. Bonnet House, Fort Lauderdale
6. Casa Vecchia, Fort Lauderdale
7. Chart House Restaurant, Fort Lauderdale
8. Stranahan House, Fort Lauderdale
9. King-Cromartie House, Fort Lauderdale
10. Wagner Homestead, Miami
11. Vizcaya Museum and Gardens, Miami
12. Barnacle, Coconut Grove, Miami
13. Merrick House, Coral Gables

SOUTH FLORIDA

Tracks to Miami

In the mid-19th century, North Florida and the area around the St. Johns River were rapidly becoming important centers for agriculture and tourism. Key West was flourishing as a capital for salvaging wrecked ships. But the eastern coast and southern tip of the mainland were still largely wilderness.

Its few settlers contended with severe hardships, which ranged from heat and humidity to hostile Seminoles, who gradually had been pushed further into the swampy Everglades as civilization advanced south. Even remaining in touch with the rest of the world was difficult for those hardy souls living in South Florida. In the 1880s, the sparsely settled area that now is Miami was so remote that it took "barefoot mailmen" three days to hike and row in from Jupiter, 90 miles to the north, with letters and packages.

At that time, Dade County stretched all the way north to Jupiter and included part of Lake Okeechobee, near the equally undeveloped Lake Worth area.

But by the 1890s, when Henry Flagler pushed his railroad south of St. Augustine and on into Fort Pierce and Palm Beach, the picture changed dramatically. Flagler had received permission to extend his tracks as far south as present-day Miami in 1892, but he had stopped at Palm Beach in 1894 and built his magnificent resort hotels.

The ambitious Julia Tuttle, who owned 644 acres of woods and marshland north of the Miami River, had tried to persuade Flagler to connect her land with the rest of the east coast. She had no luck, until the disastrous freeze of 1894-95, which destroyed the citrus crop even south of Palm Beach. With the withering of the trees, the flow of tourists to fabulous Palm Beach slowed.

So when Mrs. Tuttle sent Flagler a branch of fresh orange blossoms from the still-warm south, he pushed on through, arriving in Fort Dallas in 1896. To the South Florida town — which was then a dozen sand trails that had been cut through dense palmetto, mangroves and sea grapes — Flagler brought more than a train and the first hotel.

As part of his agreement with Mrs. Tuttle and her wealthy neighbors, the William Brickells, he also paved roads, founded an electric company, built a waterworks and sewage system and helped create the first school, hospital and newspaper in South Florida. Some citizens wanted to name the new city Flagler, in honor of its benefactor, but he declined.

As civilization rushed to a Miami now linked to Palm Beach, St. Augustine and points north, its character quickly changed. Incorporated three months after Flagler and his train arrived in 1896, the city was named Miami — perhaps derived from an Indian word for "sweet water" or "big water." It soon became a boom city.

Biscayne Bay and the edge of the Everglades were drained. Residential and tourist developments such as George Merrick's Coral Gables, Glenn Curtiss' Opa-Locka — and, during the Depression, the fabulous home of Florida's art deco hotels, Miami Beach — were quickly begun.

During the boom years, Palm Beach was developing along grander and more lavish, if equally fanciful, lines. The creator of the city's distinctive architecture, Addison Mizner, arrived in Palm Beach in 1918, and set about persuading wealthy visitors to Flagler's hotel that they could have their own mansions for the season. He offered captivating houses in Mediterranean styles — Spanish, Moorish and Italian, especially Venetian — that looked perfect for the locale.

Mizner's fanciful, flamboyant designs in Palm Beach and, slightly later, in Boca Raton, made a permanent imprint on Florida's architecture. For decades, buildings by such noted architects and developers as James Gamble Rogers in Winter Park, George Merrick in Coral Gables and, just a few years ago, Philip Johnson in Miami were designed in the Spanish style that Mizner made famous.

GILBERT'S BAR HOUSE OF REFUGE

This shingled, two-story house — which overlooks the Atlantic Ocean from Hutchinson Island near Stuart — is one of 10 structures that once sheltered survivors of shipwrecks along Florida's east coast. The house ironically was named for Don Pedro Gilbert, a notorious pirate who operated on the waterways in the area during the early 19th century.

The shelter opened on Dec. 1, 1876, under the care of keeper Fred Whitehead. He patrolled the beaches for the state during storms and lived in the trim, functional building for a salary of $40 a month.

The house's four ground-floor rooms — a bedroom, living room, dining room and kitchen, with a storage area attached — stand side by side without hallways. The open dormitory for rescued sailors on the second floor is reached by a staircase to one side of the living room. A wide porch encloses the simply arranged rooms, providing protection from sun and rain while allowing breezes to enter the many windows and circulate through the house.

The house sheltered shipwreck survivors for nearly 70 years. Among the more spectacular nearby wrecks was that of the 767-ton Georges Valentine, which went aground 500 yards east of the house in 1904. The ship was carrying $17,000 worth of lumber, which was salvaged and used in a variety of local buildings, and its survivors were sheltered in the house on Gilbert's Bar. The wreck at times can still be seen from the house, which is the only one of the original nine shelters still standing.

The house served through the Spanish-American War and the first and second world wars before being deactivated in 1945. It sat, abandoned, until 1953, when the structure and its 16.8-acre site were purchased by Martin County for $168. The oldest standing structure in the county, the house was restored in 1975 and opened as a historical museum.

Its period furnishings include an old-fashioned kitchen, complete with the restored 1876 fireplace and cast-iron pans, a Victorian settee and tilt-top candlestand made between 1780 and 1830. Rows of cots in the upstairs dormitory appear ready to greet survivors, and at the foot of each, a blanket is neatly folded. The keeper's downstairs bedroom features a mahogany spool bed and handwoven coverlet, both from the early to mid-19th century, and a sampler stitched in 1880 by a 10-year-old girl.

Gilbert's Bar House of Refuge, Hutchinson Island, between Fort Pierce and Stuart, is open from 1 p.m. to 4:25 p.m. Tuesday through Sunday. An admission is charged. For further information, call (407) 225-1875.

FLORIDA HISTORIC HOMES

DUBOIS HOUSE

The shingle-style Dubois House overlooking Jupiter Inlet was built by Harry Dubois for his bride in the late 1890s. He had come to Florida from New Jersey in 1887.

When he met Susan Saunders, a Palm Beach schoolteacher, on a blind date and married her, Dubois purchased land to build a home. She had told him that she wanted to be able to see the water from her windows. Their property lay on a 20-foot-high, 90-foot-long Jaega Indian shell mound, and over the years the family sold shell rock from the ancient mound.

The couple's first house was small, and by the time the four children were born, it had become so cramped that Dubois decided to expand it.

To the living room, dining room, bedroom and kitchen — which, typically for Southern frame structures, stood apart from the living quarters — he added three bedrooms and a bathroom in 1903. To do so, he raised the roof and placed a "grandparents" room and the children's rooms on the new second story.

Lighting in the house was by kerosene lamp. Cypress walls were unpainted, and red-painted floors

were covered with handmade rag rugs. The windows had no curtains, for there were no neighbors around. But during the warm months when mosquitos and sand fleas were a problem, sheer cotton fabric was tacked over the windows, and every morning they were swept off with a palmetto broom. A palmetto broom was also kept by the door so that those entering the house could brush bugs off their clothes.

Today, although its walls have been painted, the Dubois House is much as it looked in the early years of the century. One change is the coquina rock fireplace, which was built in the 1930s at the request of a couple who rented the house from Susan after Harry's death. The fireplace was constructed of coquina rocks found on the nearby beach.

The house is owned by Palm Beach County and is operated by the Loxahatchee Historical Society. Many of its furnishings have been donated by family members. The rugs made by Susan and her daughter Anna are on the wooden floors. One bedroom holds a Dubois commode set, and the old Dubois dining set graces the dining room. The Bahama bed belonged to Harry, and the piano is the one that was used by the Duboises.

In addition, friends of the Dubois family donated such period objects as a treadle sewing machine, a kerosene lamp and a food safe. Among other furnishings are an oak table from an old house that stood nearby but has been replaced by condominiums.

The Dubois House, in Dubois Park in Jupiter on the south side of the Jupiter Inlet, is open 1 to 3 p.m. Sundays. No admission is charged. For further information, call (407) 747-6639.

SOUTH FLORIDA

LA VIEILLE MAISON

The elegant La Vieille Maison restaurant was built in 1928 in the Mediterranean style so popular in the Florida boom years.

Built on the outer reaches of legendary architect Addison Mizner's Boca Raton Club, the house supposedly was the home of his chief engineer and may have been intended as a model home for a Mizner-inspired residential project. There is some controversy about the house's designer; some sources believe it was Mizner.

The two-story stucco house has secluded courtyards and Mediterranean-style balconies, arched alcoves, a stucco fireplace framed with ceramic tiles, floors of both oak hardwood and clay tile, and an elaborate stone fountain.

To enter the restaurant, guests walk through huge wrought-iron gates into lush tropical gardens.

On the exterior, round-top windows are articulated by heavy moldings and a single column that stands between each set of double windows.

Terra-cotta tiles on the gently pitched roofs add to the Mediterranean tone of the house, as do rough-hewn beams and brightly colored, boldly patterned Spanish and Portuguese tiles inside. The tiles were purchased by the present owners from the Palm Beach importer who supplied tile to Mizner.

Over the years, the house has undergone a number of structural changes, serving as an apartment building and before that, the home of the Belgian Countess d'Aultremont, who lived there for a time with her mother and brother.

A real estate and travel agency had offices in the building when it was bought in 1975 by its current owners, Leonce Picot and Al Kocab. They received permission from the city of Boca Raton to restore the home to the Mediterranean style that is typical of Mizner.

The interior of the restaurant features dining rooms on both floors — the former living room is the main dining room — and, weather permitting, guests can be seated on balconies overlooking the courtyard.

Picot and Kocab have furnished La Vieille Maison and their Casa Vecchia restaurant in Fort Lauderdale with antiques and antique reproductions that make up an eclectic blend of styles and periods, including Jacobean English, French and Victorian. Among the antiques are a large collection of chandeliers and sconces.

La Vieille Maison specializes in dishes of the French Provence and Riviera, with a few selections from Italy.

Seatings at La Vieille Maison, 770 E. Palmetto Park Road in Boca Raton, are 6, 6:30 and 9, and 9:30 p.m. For details, call (407) 421-7370.

FLORIDA HISTORIC HOMES

WHITEHALL

In 1902, the year after Whitehall was built, the *New York Herald* described the house as "more wonderful than any palace in Europe, grander and more magnificent than any other private dwelling in the world."

Railroad-and-hotel magnate Henry Flagler built Whitehall for his young bride, Mary Lily Kenan. Their lavish residence, also described as the Taj Mahal of North America, was designed by New York architects Carrere and Hastings. The firm also was responsible for the U.S. Senate building, the Frick Mansion and the New York Public Library. Whitehall's construction cost of $2.5 million didn't include its furnishings, which added another $1.5 million to the total.

Nor does the price tag truly give a sense of Whitehall's glory.

Set on a 6-acre site bordering Lake Worth in Palm Beach, the 55,000-square-foot mansion is surrounded by a wrought-iron fence and gardens of palms, hibiscus, orange trees and other native plantings, as well as exotic vegetation from around the world. Whitehall is entered through a set of double bronze doors that were never locked when the Flaglers lived there, because a pair of uniformed doorboys were always on duty.

Inside is the Marble Entrance Hall, which is 110 feet long and 40 feet wide. Its walls, floors and 16 columns are made of seven types of marble. The benches and urns on the landing of the double staircase are of Carrara marble.

The ceiling's painted-canvas panels, which symbolize Prosperity and Happiness, flank a 20-foot dome that shows "The Crowning of Knowledge." Continuing the classical theme are the medallions, massive gilded moldings and plaster figures throughout the room. A vast millefleurs Kerman carpet covers the floor. Gold Louis XIV-style furniture stands in the hall, which the Flaglers used as a reception area and, occasionally, for entertaining guests.

Among other rooms furnished with impressive antiques are the Italian Renaissance Library, decorated in the style of the early 16th century; the Louis XIV Music Room; the "Swiss" Billiards Room; the Louis XV Ballroom; the Elizabethan Breakfast Room; the Francis I Dining Room; and the Louis XVI Salon.

The most elaborate of the 15 bedroom suites is that of the Flaglers, although such rooms as the Yellow Roses and Modern English are charming. The master bedroom is decorated in the Louis XV style, with gold silk moire damask wallhangings and draperies. The two-tone pearl-gray furniture, which is mounted in gilded bronze, has never left Whitehall. Mrs. Flagler's dressing room, next to the bedroom, now contains glass-fronted cabinets of items from the Flagler museum's costume collection. Also adjacent is the 17-by-11-foot marble bathroom, with its green onyx sinks, sunken bathtub, open shower and maple housings for its fixtures.

Construction of the three-story mansion took 18 months. Between the 1902 winter season and May 1913, when Flagler died, the couple entertained many of the great figures of their day there. Among the guests were opera stars Nellie Melba and Enrico Caruso, Admiral and Mrs. George Dewey, Woodrow Wilson, Elihu Root, John Jacob Astor and the Duke and Duchess of Manchester.

Before the arrival of Flagler's railroad — and the resort hotels and tourists that immediately followed — Palm Beach was little more than a wilderness. But by the mid-1890s, when the gigantic Royal Poinciana Hotel and The Breakers opened, it had become the country's most fashionable winter gathering space. Whitehall stands as a supreme monument to the Gilded Age.

Whitehall (the Henry Morrison Flagler Museum), Coconut Row and Whitehall Way in Palm Beach, is open 10 a.m. to 5 p.m. Tuesday through Saturday, noon to 5 p.m. Sunday. An admission is charged. For further information, call (407) 655-2833.

FLORIDA HISTORIC HOMES

BONNET HOUSE

When Frederic Bartlett built his Bonnet House in Fort Lauderdale between 1920 and 1921, the home was in a quiet, sleepy community. Today, the mansion sits in the middle of a sprawling city, an oasis in a bustling resort.

Set on a 35-acre site with 700 feet fronting the Atlantic Ocean, the two-story structure was a winter residence for the amateur architect and his first wife. Bartlett built the 30-room home of native coral stone, Dade County pine and concrete blocks that were poured on the site. He imported the second-floor balcony rail from New Orleans, giving the house a Creole look. And later, when bonnet lilies bloomed on the pond near the entrance, Bartlett found a name for his house.

But it wasn't until Frederic married his second wife that the white house developed its present whimsical character. Both he and his new wife, Evelyn, were artists. They displayed in their winter residence not only their own work and a variety of collectibles, but also such tropical flora and fauna as orchids, parrots and monkeys. Secluded behind high concrete walls and iron gates, the Bartletts and their guests could watch black swans on the lake in front of the porch.

Inside the elaborate entrance gate that Bartlett designed is the courtyard around which the house was built. A coral fountain plays in its center, and is surrounded by palms and other lush tropical plantings. The aviary Frederic built for Evelyn is also in the courtyard, and nearby stands his studio. The studio (the first building on the estate) features a high, beamed ceiling, a two-story window that admits the northern light artists so admire, Bartlett's art works and even his original palettes.

In the house, next to the wood-paneled dining room, are a Spartan pantry and kitchen. Mounted fish and sea-turtle skulls cover the walls, and china is displayed in three cabinets, along with Frederic's collection of beer steins. In the portico that leads from the dining room to Evelyn's suite is a mural of a Haitian shoreline, with shells pressed into concrete archways and obelisk shapes in the corners.

Other features of the Bonnet House are its shell museum, a round room in which sets of matched shells found on the beach are shown in cases that line the walls; a bamboo bar where lime cocktails were served; an orchid house; and a music room with a 14-foot-high ceiling and a floor painted to look like marble.

Evelyn Bartlett willed the $35 million estate to the Florida Trust for Historic Preservation in 1983. It is the most valuable property owned by any state historical society. She occupies the house during the winter months, so tours are offered only between May and December.

Tours of the Bonnet House, 900 N. Birch Road in Fort Lauderdale, are given at 10 a.m. and 1:30 p.m. Tuesdays and Thursdays, and 1:30 p.m. on Sundays between May and December. An admission is charged. For reservations, call (305) 563-5393.

SOUTH FLORIDA

FLORIDA HISTORIC HOMES

CASA VECCHIA

Casa Vecchia, the well-known restaurant on Fort Lauderdale's Intracoastal Waterway, was built by the heirs of the Pond's Cold Cream fortune between 1936 and 1938.

The two-story Spanish Revival structure was also, in the early '50s, home of Stephen O'Connell and his wife. O'Connell served from 1955 to 1967 as a justice of the Florida Supreme Court (briefly in 1967 as chief justice) and from 1967 to 1973 as the chancellor of the University of Florida.

Among the house's architectural features are a sloping, terra-cotta tile roof, large bay windows, round-topped windows and arched doorways.

Although the house has been remodeled to incorporate 12 additional rooms, its interior retains the feeling of an elegant Spanish villa with high, beamed ceilings, a huge, hooded stucco fireplace, and floors of Spanish clay tiles or oak planks.

Renovations include the addition of two enclosed balconies that overlook the waterway, and one balcony that opens off a former bedroom and extends into the branches of the courtyard's giant melaleuca tree. Greenhouse-like downstairs additions house dining rooms surrounded by the lushly landscaped tropical courtyard.

The house has a varied collection of antique light fixtures and furnishings in an eclectic blend of periods, and English and French styles.

Casa Vecchia, 209 N. Birch Road in Fort Lauderdale, specializes in northern Italian cuisine. The restaurant serves from 6 p.m. until 10:30 p.m. From Dec. 15 to Mothers Day, seatings are on the half hour. For further information, call (305) 463-7575.

WAGNER HOMESTEAD

Miami's oldest house has survived hurricanes, wars, booms and busts and — perhaps most difficult — recent progress, Florida style. The simple raised structure in Miami's Lummus Park is the only example of a pioneer home that remains from South Florida's early homesteading years.

Even the briefest glance at bustling Miami makes it difficult to imagine the wilderness that William Wagner found when he arrived in 1855.

Wagner, a veteran of the Mexican War, was following his former military unit when he came to Florida. He had met and married his French-Creole wife, Eveline DeBau, in Charleston, S.C., and left most of his family in South Carolina while he made his first trip to the area. His unit had reopened Fort Dallas (now Miami), and Wagner had set up a store at the fort for the soldiers. Just up the river on the banks of what is now Wagner Creek, he built his two-room frame home and mill. His family later joined him.

Most of their neighbors tended to be transients or settlers who became discouraged at the hardships they met in the hot, insect-ridden river community. But the Wagners stuck it out. They were, by all accounts, solid citizens who were honest and dependable. In a rapidly changing society, and a sometimes threatening environment, the Wagners became pillars of early Miami.

Early settlers faced occasional raids from hostile Seminole Indians, who had been pushed into the Everglades by white settlement. During the mid-19th century, soldiers were still trying to exterminate the Seminoles. The Wagners, however, were among the first to establish cordial relations with their Seminole neighbors and entertained some of that nation's legendary leaders in their home.

The Wagners were hosts to many prominent and controversial guests — soldiers from both the Union and the Confederacy, some of the era's most notorious carpetbaggers and such prominent figures as the William Brickells and Julia Tuttle. As the city grew around them, the Wagners stayed where they had first settled in their simple, steep-roofed house. Eveline was buried on the property near a church erected by the family, and William — who lived until 1901, long enough to see Flagler's railroad arrive and transform Miami — lies in Miami City Cemetery.

Threatened with demolition, the Wagner house was acquired by the Dade Heritage Trust in 1979 and moved from its site to Lummus Park. It has been structurally restored but remains unfurnished.

The Wagner Homestead in Miami is open only by special arrangement with the Dade Heritage Trust, 190 S.E. 12th Terrace, Miami, Fla. 33131. For further information, call (305) 358-9572.

FLORIDA HISTORIC HOMES

SOUTH FLORIDA

CHART HOUSE RESTAURANT

The two, two-story houses that now form the Chart House Restaurant in Fort Lauderdale were built around 1904 by Philemon Bryan, a pioneer.

Made of poured concrete blocks that had been molded on the site, the houses were built for Bryan's two sons, Thomas and Reed. Philemon and his older son, Thomas, had come to Fort Lauderdale in 1895 to help cut the right-of-way for Henry Flagler's Florida East Coast Railway Co., which was then making its way to Miami.

At that time, most of South Florida was a dense, swampy tangle of subtropical vegetation infested with mosquitos and other insects, as well as reptiles. Most would not have considered Fort Lauderdale a promising place to build, but the Bryans stayed on and were responsible for developing the city.

They created the first neighborhood in Fort Lauderdale, and among the roads they created were Las Olas and Sunrise boulevards. They also are credited with developing the first power plant, telephone exchange, bank and ice company. The older Bryan brother, Thomas, served as city councilman, city commissioner and state representative. Reed became president of the city's Board of Trade and was at one time mayor of Fort Lauderdale.

The two houses had acetylene lighting when they were new, provided by the Davis Acetylene Co. (next to the King-Cromartie House). They had pine floors and brick fireplaces. Their sewage and irrigation systems were on the property, as were the vegetable gardens in which food for the families was grown. By 1913, a boat house had been constructed on the New River for the Bryans, although the boathouse has since been demolished.

During the 1940s, the Reed Bryan house was converted into a duplex, and later into five units. His brother's house remained a single-family dwelling, and acquired additions that have since been removed.

Both houses changed hands several times before 1975, and the Reed Bryan house was extensively damaged by fire in 1980. Fortunately, its block construction made it somewhat fireproof, and its skeleton survived the fire. The house was reconstructed, and in 1981 both of the Bryan houses were completely renovated by the city, which had made them the focal point of a historical district in 1975. The city now leases the building to the Chart House Restaurant's operators.

The Chart House Restaurant (the Bryan Homes) is at 301 Southwest Third Ave. in Fort Lauderdale. It serves American-style cuisine. For further information, call (305) 523-0177.

FLORIDA HISTORIC HOMES

STRANAHAN HOUSE

The two-story, frame house on the banks of the New River in Fort Lauderdale was built in 1901 as a general store and public hall. Frank Stranahan's business served the young, rapidly growing community and its many Seminole Indian residents.

On the first floor was the store, and on the second level was the public hall, which was reached by an exterior staircase. Weekly dances and other festivities were held there. The wide verandas that shade the walls on two floors provided sleeping places for Indians who traded at the store.

By 1906, however, Stranahan's business had become so successful that it had outgrown the building and was moved to a larger structure. Frank and Ivy Cromartie Stranahan — the schoolteacher he had married in 1900 at her Lemon City home — renovated the store and made it their home. They added bay windows to the south, or riverfront, side of the 2,000-square-foot structure.

The Stranahans added a fireplace and chimney, the house's only source of heat, and put in gas lighting fixtures. They changed the partitioning of the first floor to conform to its new use as a residence. It's thought that the Stranahans left the second floor undivided until about 1913, when they also built an interior stairway to the upper level.

The house's first kitchen was separate from the house; it's likely that they constructed a kitchen inside, in a room that was originally used as a dining room, in 1913. About that time, the Stranahans also had the house wired for electricity and added indoor plumbing.

By 1915, the Stranahan's frontier mansion in the South Florida pine flatlands had acquired a water tower and tanks. In its heyday, it was the center of Fort Lauderdale's social life, and was the setting for dinner parties for Henry Flagler and other notables.

During those parties, fiddlers and accordionists provided entertainment for the guests, who often were friends stopping by on their way to the new resort city of Miami. When the Florida land boom failed in the late 1920s, Stranahan's business suffered, and in 1929 he took his own life in the nearby New River.

His widow, however, continued to live in the house until she died in 1971, at the age of 91. As time passed, additions obscured its original outlines. The first floor was rented to tenants who used it as a tearoom and restaurant. During the winter, paying guests lived on the second floor. Ivy Stranahan added small dormers to the roof for ventilation and moved into the attic.

In 1979, the same year the last restaurant that used the house closed, the house was listed on the National Register of Historic Places. Between 1981 and 1984, the various expansions were removed and the house was restored to its 1915 appearance. It opened to the public in 1984.

The Stranahan House is on Las Olas Boulevard at the New River Tunnel in Fort Lauderdale. Hours are 10 a.m. to 4 p.m. Wednesday, Friday and Saturday, 1 to 4 p.m. Sunday. An admission is charged. For further information, call (305) 463-4374.

FLORIDA HISTORIC HOMES

VIZCAYA MUSEUM AND GARDENS

Vizcaya is one of Florida's grandest homes, an elaborate Italian Renaissance palazzo-style mansion that overlooks Biscayne Bay.

The gracious villa may be approached through a pristine 10-acre formal garden. The garden re-creates a 17th century Italian hill garden, and it has fragrant plantings, gazebos, pools, grottoes, mazes, sculptures, cascades and fountains. Australian pines have been shaped into fanciful topiary designs.

It took 1,000 workers two years to build the $15 million, 70-room mansion that James Deering named Vizcaya, the Basque word for elevated place. Vizcaya's walls are stone and stucco, and its clay-tiled roof is punctuated by chimneys, spires and sculpted figures.

On the villa's eastern facade, the high, arched windows of the loggia open onto a plaza that descends by a series of steps to Biscayne Bay. There, in the bay, a stone barge decorated with sculpture and pruned plantings serves as a breakwater.

The wonders of Vizcaya don't end at its doors. Inside the 34 halls and rooms that are open to the public are countless priceless works of art. Among them are tapestries, furnishings, Oriental carpets, moldings and other architectural elements that Deering found on his many trips to Europe. The pieces range in origin from first century Rome to 15th century Spain and Italy. They include cedar-and-bronze doors from Torlonio Palace in Rome, intricate inlaid-wood chairs from Combe Abbey, England, and a 16th century tapestry from Tournai, Belgium, that once belonged to poet Robert Browning.

Signs of opulence are everywhere. In the master bedroom, silken walls rise to a ceiling decorated with gilded, molded garlands, and the bed draperies are supported by a French Empire-style eagle. Silver moldings in the shape of plaques stud the marble walls of the master bath, in which two sets of tub faucets once controlled flows of fresh- or saltwater.

Deering, a bachelor, lived in the palazzo until his death in 1925, and his estate remained in the possession of his heirs until 1952. That year, it was given to the county and became the Dade County Art Museum. It now is the Vizcaya Museum and Gardens. Narrated, self-guided, and evening sound-and-light tours are available. A walk through the house and gardens takes about three hours.

The Vizcaya Museum and Gardens, 3252 S. Miami Ave., Miami, is open from 9:30 a.m. to 5 p.m. daily except Christmas. An admission is charged and there are reduced prices for senior citizens and children. For further information, call (305) 579-2813.

FLORIDA HISTORIC HOMES

CORAL GABLES HOUSE

This plantation house was the boyhood home of George Merrick, founder of the city of Coral Gables. The house was built about 1906 of a local fossil-bearing limestone that, according to legend, the Merricks mistook for coral.

The two-story, six-bedroom Coral Gables House replaced the frame structure that the young George and his Congregational minister father, the Rev. Solomon Merrick, had constructed. They had built that first house when they arrived in South Florida from Massachusetts, in 1899, to grow fruit and vegetables.

Designed by George's mother, Althea, Coral Gables House shows a fine adaption of a sedate, classical New England style to a new climate and a new set of building materials. A graceful Palladian window is set into a triangular area over the roof of the broad, ground-level porch, and a small pediment over the columned entryway repeats the shape of the roofline.

The building materials Mrs. Merrick chose for her home were practical and readily available: oolitic limestone and durable Dade County pine for the house itself, and concrete for the columns that support the porch. The house was raised above the ground to allow cross-ventilation and to protect it from flooding. Its steeply pitched, gabled roof featured a coral-colored tile.

When the Rev. Merrick and his son arrived in Florida, they converted their 160-acre pinewood wilderness into a garden. The family had spent its life savings — $1,100 — to buy the land. After cultivating it, the Merricks became the largest exporters of grapefruit in the Southeast.

Mrs. Merrick and her four younger children arrived in Florida after the reverend and George.

They not only built the new plantation house but also set up a school in an old log cabin on the property, calling it the Guavonia School after the guava that grew there.

Coral Gables has been restored and is decorated with period furnishings from the 1920s, many of which belonged to the Merrick family. Among them are the baby grand player piano, the hall tree, and the dining room and bedroom sets.

The Coral Gables House, 907 Coral Way in Coral Gables, is open from 1 to 4 p.m. Wednesday and Sunday. An admission is charged. For further information, call (305) 442-6593.

SOUTH FLORIDA

KING-CROMARTIE HOUSE

The two-story frame house was built in 1907 for Edwin Thomas King. He came to Fort Lauderdale from New Smyrna in 1895, just after the terrible freeze that killed crops all the way to south of Palm Beach in the winter of 1894-95. The next year, King's wife, Susan, and their four children arrived on the first passenger train to reach Fort Lauderdale.

King, who planted citrus groves and a pineapple field, is best known as the building contractor who developed the hollow concrete block. He constructed many of Fort Lauderdale's buildings, among them the first two schoolhouses, the first courthouse and the New River Inn. He also brought the first schoolteacher, Ivy Cromartie (later Mrs. Frank Strahanan) to Fort Lauderdale.

The King-Cromartie House is the second one built by King for his family; the first was sold. The 1907 house, which was made of Dade County pine, was originally a one-story structure. It was on the south bank of the New River, to the west of Frank and Ivy Cromartie Stranahan's trading post and house. The Kings' two-bedroom house had the city's first indoor plumbing and acetylene lighting. Beneath the house was a well from which water was pumped into the house. When electricity became available, in 1911, King installed fixtures in each room. That same year, he also built a second floor on the house, adding two bedrooms and a bathroom.

The beams below the house are made of wood salvaged from ships wrecked off the coast. The house is furnished with early 20th century pieces, among them Susan King's treadle sewing machine. The house has chairs that could be ordered from the Sears & Roebuck catalog for 37 cents each, and an oak icebox of the sort that was stocked with ice from Miami every day. The piano in the living room was the first in the city, and originally was used in the local Methodist church.

The last family member to occupy the house was Louise King Cromartie, a daughter of Edwin and Susan King. She lived in it with her husband, Bloxham A. Cromartie, the younger brother of Ivy Cromartie Stranahan.

In 1971, the Junior League of Fort Lauderdale moved the house to its current location, and had it restored. The city now owns it.

The King-Cromartie House is part of the Discovery Center, 231 S.W. Second Ave., Fort Lauderdale. There is an admission to the center. House tours are Tuesday through Friday at varying times in the afternoon. For further information, call (305) 462-4116.

FLORIDA HISTORIC HOMES

THE BARNACLE

When Ralph Middleton Monroe first visited South Florida in 1877 at the age of 25, the area was still largely a wilderness. But the Staten Island native's sympathies lay with Ralph Waldo Emerson and the transcendentalist movement's love of nature and adherence to the simple life. So he chose to return south five years later with his wife and her sister.

Mrs. Monroe suffered from tuberculosis, and the trip by steamer to Key West and then by small sailboat into Biscayne Bay was difficult. She died while they were camped along the river. Her sister died on the trip back north.

Monroe wintered in Florida for seven years before deciding to move here permanently. He settled in Coconut Grove in 1889 and built his home in keeping with transcendentalist principles, creating his own Walden Pond in Florida.

The Barnacle reflects its designer's beliefs, as well as his experience as a ship's builder. Its style is simple and direct, in tune with its site and climate. It was originally a one-story Dade County pine structure that stood eight steps above the ground for cross-ventilation and protection from flooding. So that it would survive hurricanes, Monroe anchored the Barnacle to sunken pilings of pine treated with crude oil to preserve it.

And, so that he could be an Emersonian "man in the open air," he planned the house as a comfortable, open place that would exist harmoniously with its lush surroundings of tropical plantings. A veranda wraps around three sides of the house, offering shelter from sun and showers while allowing windows to be kept open. Four corner rooms surround a central, octagonal dining room that features a skylight. When the skylight is open, breezes flow throughout the house.

By 1908, Monroe had remarried and become the father of two children. The house had become cramped. To provide more space, he raised the older structure and added a new ground floor. The Barnacle became a two-story house. Monroe lived in it until his death in 1933. His descendants occupied it until 1973, then sold it to the state so that a portion of old Florida could be preserved.

The interior of the 11-room house, finished on the first floor with plaster and on the second with pine paneling, contains many of the late-19th century furnishings Monroe brought with him from his home in New York. Other furnishings include two 16th century European chairs given to Monroe by his across-Biscayne Bay neighbor, James Deering, owner of the elegant Vizcaya.

The Barnacle is at 3485 Main Highway in Coconut Grove. Tours are scheduled at 9 a.m., 10:30 a.m., 1 p.m. and 2:30 p.m. Thursday through Monday. An admission is charged. For further information, call (305) 448-9445.

CHAPTER VII

THE KEYS

FLORIDA HISTORIC HOMES

Zone VI:
THE KEYS

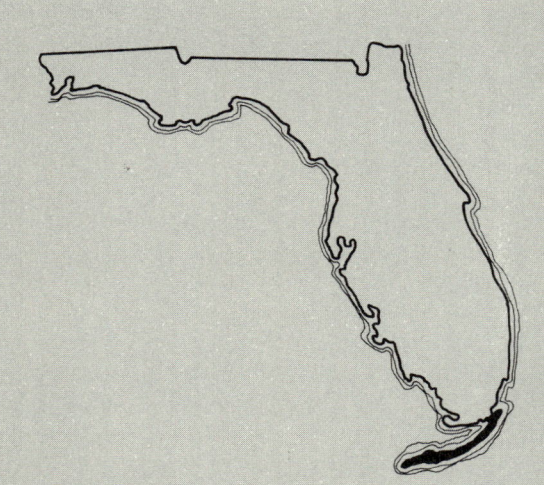

1. Oldest House (Wrecker's Museum), Key West
2. Audubon House, Key West
3. Ernest Hemingway House, Key West
4. Matheson House, Lignumvitae Key
5. Curry Mansion, Key West
6. Artist House, Key West
7. Eaton Lodge, Key West
8. Gideon Lowe House, Key West
9. Louie's Backyard Restaurant, Key West

Treasures in the Tropics

Key West and the other small islands that are just south of the peninsula and north of the Florida Straits are not at all typical of the rest of the state.

The islands were founded on a seafaring, salvaging economy rather than on agriculture or tourism. They are at a very low elevation — Key West is just 4 feet above sea level — and their climate and vegetation are more tropical than the rest of Florida.

Just as this region is different, so is its architecture. The architecture that evolved in Key West shows great ingenuity and willingness to synthesize various traditions and indigenous materials.

In 1803, the United States acquired the Louisiana Territory from France, and developed ports along the gulf coast.

These new ports could be reached only through the Florida Straits, one of the busiest shipping routes in the world — and one of the most dangerous. Among the hazards facing captains were the currents, weather and shallow waters over the coral of the Florida Reef.

Just as worrisome for shippers — and as welcome for the residents of Key West — were the 10,000 or so pirates who sailed between Cuba and Florida. Ships that escaped such legendary outlaws as Blackbeard and Black Caesar often ran out of luck near Key West, where they wrecked on the Reef.

Their cargos were seized by the so-called "wreckers" of Key West, who were able to build and furnish whole houses with their salvaged material. Some of the old houses of Key West were made with salvaged mahogany, which was far less expensive than wood brought south by boat.

Because of the unusual materials available to Key West ships' carpenters, and because of the location and climate, an eclectic style sprang up early. It was called "Conch" after the creators of the style, islanders who ate the meat of the large seashells.

These frame structures reflect many influences. Prominent is the airy Bahamian, with open porches, hinged and louvered shutters and encircling verandas on one or two levels. From New Orleans came filigreed trellises and balustrades. Widows' walks on the roofs, usually steeply peaked, show an awareness of New England styles. And many residences have profiles and details that draw from the dominant Greek and Gothic revivals that swept the nation during Key West's heyday, which ended about the time of the Civil War.

Because of the constant threat of hurricanes, many Key West homes were anchored to the island's underlying coral rock with cypress posts. The wooden building materials may not have been particularly sturdy, but the construction techniques of the Key West houses allowed them to withstand strong winds and waves. Their sills were pegged to the posts that held them in place, and their joints were made without nails, using mortise-and-tenon construction that is beautifully crafted and amazingly durable.

The islanders continued to prosper even after Florida became a territory, in 1821, and federal authorities sought to curb its wrecking activities. Still, in 1855, wrecking brought in millions of dollars in revenue. At that time, the 2-by-4-mile city was the most populous in the state, and only the Civil War and the Union blockade of Florida's ports slowed the wrecking-based economy. Near the end of the 19th century, it had become a cigar-making center, and many small, wooden structures date from Key West's second period of prosperity.

Those small, functional houses are very different from the eclectic homes of the wreckers, but show an equal facility for adapting to the region. Most are in the so-called "shotgun" style, in which rooms open off a hallway that runs the length of the narrow, rectangular structures. By the end of the century, however, much of the cigar-making industry had shifted to Tampa. In the 1920s, Key West began attracting creative people like Ernest Hemingway. By the 1960s, it had become a haven for authors like Tennessee Williams and Thomas McGuane.

OLDEST HOUSE

This simple frame house, which now is the Wrecker's Museum in Key West, probably was built around 1829 and is the oldest in the city. One of its earliest owners — and perhaps its builder — was a jack-of-all-trades named Richard Cussons. He had come north from Nassau in the Bahamas around 1828 and may never actually have lived in the house.

In Key West, Cussons became a carpenter, grocer and auctioneer. During his early years in the city his two-story, Dade County pine structure was probably at the corner of Whitehead and Caroline streets. At some point, it was moved to its present site on Duval Street, where it presumably was added to another house.

It became the home of a merchant seaman and wrecker, Capt. Francis B. Watlington, around 1829. Born in the Virgin Islands, Watlington had come to Key West from New York with his 16-year-old bride around 1828, and moved into the then-new Oldest House soon afterward. Watlington replaced the clapboard house's roof scuttles — or ship's hatches — with three dormer windows, which were graduated in size. All of the house's windows were shuttered to protect them from stormy weather.

Like other residences of its period and later, the Oldest House shows a variety of influences, not the least of which is that of a ship's carpenter. There is a ship's hatch on the roof and a "landlubber's tilt" — a crooked wall and window — in the captain's office. The building is raised 3 feet from the ground on lime-rock piers for air circulation. Its kitchen, which stands about 12 feet from the house to keep the heat generated there from the rest of the main wooden structure, has an open fireplace and a wall oven. This outside kitchen is the only original one still standing in the Keys.

The simple cottage-type house was planned around a long hall that opens into two front parlors, with a dining room on one side and a bedroom (now used as a caretaker's quarters) on the other. Off the porch is the captain's office, opposite another bedroom that is closed to the public. Most of the Oldest House's nine rooms are decorated with 19th century furnishings and a variety of objects from Key West history, and many of the objects are original to the house. Among them are antique toys and an 1850s, Conch-style dollhouse scaled 1 inch to 1 foot.

The Oldest House (now the Wrecker's Museum), 322 Duval St. in Key West, is open from 10 a.m. to 4 p.m. daily. An admission is charged. For further information, call (305) 294-9502.

FLORIDA HISTORIC HOMES

AUDUBON HOUSE MUSEUM

When naturalist-artist John James Audubon visited the Florida Keys in 1832, he spent time sketching in the garden of a successful harbor pilot and wrecker, Capt. John Geiger. Geiger's pleasant, Bahamian-style clapboard home had been built for the salvager's large family by ships' carpenters, and was filled with furnishings taken from cargoes of ships that had smashed on the treacherous Florida Reef.

The three-story Geiger House now is called the Audubon House Museum. It stands on a now-small lot landscaped with native plantings, but when the famous artist visited in the 1830s, the house was surrounded by gardens on a lush, 3½-acre site. The spacious grounds gave the illustrator of *Birds of America* a great deal of flora and fauna for inspiration. During his stay in the Keys, Audubon sketched 18 species of waterbirds that were new to him. Among them were the great white heron and the white-crowned pigeon, which Audubon showed on a branch of a flowering tree from the Geiger garden.

The house is as delightful as the drawings Audubon made during his visit. Its walls are of cypress and southern hardwood that had been brought in from the North. The first- and second-level porches on the front and rear of the shuttered and dormered residence offer shelter from the elements as well as access to cooling breezes.

The home's reconstructed interior is also charming. Among its prized possessions are the collection of Audubon engravings that are on view in a gallery, and fine examples of 18th and 19th century furnishings. The sitting room contains a golden harp, made in Ireland in 1790, and a Clemente spinet piano, made in 1805 and obtained from the Duchess of Bedford's estate. There also are Chippendale pieces in the dining room and master bedroom. A variety of other period objects re-create the elegance of the home's original appearance although the Geiger furniture is no longer there.

Occupied by Geiger's heirs for more than 120 years, the house was slated for demolition in 1958. Fortunately, this fine example of early Key West architecture was purchased and restored by the Wolfson Family Foundation. It is the first such project in Key West, and is maintained by the Florida Audubon Society.

Audubon House Museum, 205 Whitehead St. in Key West, is open from 9:30 a.m. to 5 p.m. daily. An admission is charged for adults and children 6-12; there is no admission for children under 6. For further information, call (305) 294-2116.

HEMINGWAY HOUSE

When Ernest Hemingway moved into the pleasant two-story, coral-stone house on Whitehead Street in Key West, the house was already 80 years old.

The house had been built in 1851 for shipper Asa Tift, and was constructed with stone found on its site. After the coral was quarried, the deep pit that remained became the basement of the Spanish Colonial structure — and at 16 feet above sea level, the Hemingway House is one of the few in Key West that has a dry cellar.

The house is surrounded by broad verandas on both floors and features tall, arched windows.

The writer and his wife, Pauline, had spent three years in rented quarters in Key West before they bought the old Tift place. After they repaired and renovated the then-decaying house, the couple and their two sons moved in.

Hemingway wrote many of his best-known works here. Among them are *A Farewell to Arms*, *To Have and Have Not*, *For Whom the Bell Tolls* and *The Snows of Kilimanjaro*.

The Hemingways traveled extensively, and on their trips found some of the house's most notewor-

thy furnishings. The carved 18th century walnut bench in a hall came from a Spanish monastery. The Moorish crystal chandelier overhead is also from Spain. The delicate chandelier over the dining table is of hand-blown Venetian glass, and the room's furnishings are 18th century Spanish. Mounted trophies from Hemingway's first Africa safari, in 1933, hang in the house, and a ceramic cat given to the author by a friend, Pablo Picas-

so, sits on a Mexican chest of drawers.

The grounds around the broad-roofed house were planted by Hemingway during the years he lived here, from 1931 to 1939. Hemingway's favorite plants still grow on the acre of land. The pool was a gift from Pauline to her husband. When he learned its price tag — $20,000 — he jokingly told her she might as well take his last penny, and pressed the coin into the concrete, where it still may be seen.

Although the marriage ended in 1939 and Hemingway moved to Cuba, Pauline continued to live in the Key West house until the writer's death in 1961. Since 1963, it has been a memorial to Hemingway — and has remained a home to dozens of what are believed to be the descendants of his cats.

The Hemingway House, 907 Whitehead St. in Key West, is open from 9 a.m. to 5 p.m. daily. An admission is charged. For further information, call (305) 294-1575.

FLORIDA HISTORIC HOMES

MATHESON HOUSE

The Matheson House and the wilderness surrounding it transport visitors to a much earlier, simpler time. A windmill that once provided power for the residence still stands on the property, and a 12,000-gallon cistern still holds fresh water channeled from the roof.

The Matheson House was built in 1919 on Lignumvitae Key for the caretaker of William J. Matheson. Matheson was a wealthy chemist who owned Lignumvitae Key and resided on another of his South Florida islands, Key Biscayne near Miami.

The Matheson House was made of Key Largo limestone, a fossil coral rock that is found on many of the upper Florida Keys. Most of the stones used on the Matheson House were collected when the 5-acre site was cleared for construction. The Dade County pine used on the building's interior is a dense, durable wood that was then readily available. The resinous pine resists insects and hurricanes, making it ideal for the location.

The house has four bedrooms, indoor plumbing, a wood-burning stove and an icebox. The house is raised about 10 feet off the ground, putting it well above sea level. Besides protecting the house from possible flooding, the elevation permits air to circulate below, keeping the house cool and keeping away mosquitos. After it was damaged in the hurricane of 1935, the house's original flat, red-tiled roof was replaced by a pitched roof shingled with cedar.

The house is furnished as it was in the late 1930s, when Capt. Abner Sweeting and his family lived in it. While he was the island's caretaker, Sweeting made 3 miles of graded trails, placed six cannons salvaged from a wreck on Carysfort Reef in the front yard as decorations, and raised a variety of animals. Among them were Mexican burros, round-ear rabbits, sacred geese and Galapagos tortoises.

The house itself is not the only attraction. Around it lies a virgin tropical forest of the kind that existed on most of Florida's upper Keys before advancing civilization scraped the thin layer of vegetation off the coral-reef islands. The exotic plants around Matheson House include mastic, strangler fig, gumbo-limbo, pigeon plum and poisonwood.

Three-hour boat tours to the house leave from Indian Key Fill on U.S. 1 at 1:30 p.m. Thursday through Monday. An admission is charged. Visitors should have walking shoes and mosquito repellent. For reservations, call (305) 664-4815.

CURRY MANSION

Very different from Key West's typical frame-house design is the ornate Curry Mansion. The house was built in 1899, long after Key West ceased being a wrecker's haven. It is an adaptation of a Paris townhouse that owner Milton Curry, son of the island's first self-made millionaire, saw on his honeymoon. The three-story, 11,000-square-foot house's 26 rooms include a front parlor, side parlor, dining room, music room, back hall, upper hall, upper rear hall, reception hall, bedrooms for family and servants and a widow's walk.

The broad porch on the clapboard house's facade is topped by a slender, neo-classical balustrade that echoes the design of the ground-level railing. In familiar Key West style, windows are shaded from sun and rain by hinged Bahama shutters. Windows in seven dormers admit light to the third level, which is reached by a broad staircase and was often used for parties.

Inside, the appointments are just as luxurious and finely detailed. The entrance hall paneling is birdseye maple, and its fretwork, columns and stair spindles are handmade. The light fixtures in the side parlor are gas and electric. Both were usual in Key West around 1900 — and both were unreliable. The buffet, carpet and glass case in the dining room are part of the house's original, astoundingly posh furnishings. Gold-colored flatware mimics the grandeur of the original Curry service for 24, which was made by Tiffany's and was solid gold.

The 1853 Chickering piano in the music room is said to have come from author Henry James' Newport house, and the lavatory fixtures were imported from China for the house's original owners. Among the wonders in the upstairs rooms are the Tiffany-style beveled glass side and fan windows in the upper hall, the 1868 cherry secretary in a guest bedroom and, in the attic, a billiard table and racks from about 1884.

The Curry Mansion, 511 Caroline St. in Key West, is open from 10 a.m. to 5 p.m. daily. An admission is charged. For further information, call (305) 294-5349.

FLORIDA HISTORIC HOMES

ARTIST HOUSE

Built between 1898 and 1900 for artist/physician Thomas Otto, the Queen Anne-style house features a wealth of colorful stylistic details. An octagonal turret rises above the frame structure's two stories, its seven shuttered casement windows admitting light to a dramatic staircase that curves around the inside of the space. Verandas wrap around the elaborate gabled structure, which is set back from the street in a small garden in typical Key West fashion.

Guests at the splendidly renovated bed-and-breakfast hotel enter through an ornate wrought-iron fence that opens onto five steps up to the pedimented doorway. Everything in the house is impressive, from 12-foot-high ceilings and tongue-in-groove Dade County pine floors, to the fancy scrollwork that crowns curving columns on the first- and second-story porches.

Thomas Otto was the son of a physician who had been a prisoner of Union soldiers at the dreaded Fort Jefferson in the Dry Tortugas. After the war, Dr. Robert Otto settled in Key West as an apothecary. His son Thomas, one of six children and also a surgeon by profession, built the imposing house on lower Eaton Street and lived in it for 40 years.

Among the house's notable features are its blend of styles, its fanciful turret, balconies, jigsaw-cut balustrade, etched-glass transoms and broad picture windows. The rooms are furnished in a restored Victorian period style, with four-poster high beds, wicker pieces and William Morris wallpapers.

Room rates at the Artist House, 534 Eaton St. in Key West, vary. For further information, call (305) 296-3977.

EATON LODGE

The three-story Greek Revival-style Eaton Lodge in Key West was built in 1886 by grocer Otis Johnson. Johnson sold the house a few years later to a Dr. Warren, whose widow lived in the house until the 1970s.

In the years the Warrens owned the house, they made several changes and additions. Warren first moved Johnson's grocery, which was next to the house, to the rear of the property, and turned it into a coach house.

Later, probably during the 1920s or '30s, as his practice prospered, Warren added a large dining room, enlarged the drawing room and added two bathrooms.

He also added rather formal 19th century-style paneling to the drawing room and dining room walls — and perhaps the beams that run the width of the 10-foot ceilings. The house's floors are polished Dade County pine.

For the most part, Eaton Lodge looks as it must have when it was new. Double doors at the entrance of the structure are surmounted by a delicate molded fan design and framed by shutters, as are its pedimented casement windows.

The lacy patterns on the railings of the house's two-story porches show a Victorian quality that contrasts pleasantly with such Greek Revival aspects as the slender, squared columns and the emphatic, pedimented facade.

The house became a bed-and-breakfast inn in 1980, when it was purchased by two Englishmen, Sam Maxwell and Denison Tempel. Tempel, an architect, planned a minor remodeling that included adding private bathrooms to each of the 11 guest rooms.

The pair redecorated the guest rooms in pastel yellow and green, and furnished them with mainly mahogany and pine English pieces of the Victorian period. Beds are old brass or painted iron.

The drawing room also boasts large American Victorian sofas, a pair of Irish Victorian chairs and collections of blue and white china.

Eaton Lodge is at 511 Eaton St. in Key West. Rooms vary seasonally in price. For further information, call (305) 294-3800.

FLORIDA HISTORIC HOMES

GIDEON LOWE HOUSE

The three-story Classic Revival frame house in Old Town Key West stands in a bricked garden with a goldfish pond. Its Bahamian features are at home with its setting among fan-palm, avocado and sour-orange trees. The small bed-and-breakfast inn — the Gideon Lowe House has six guest rooms and three bathrooms — has been restored to show the eclecticism of the island's architectural styles.

The house was begun in 1845 by the youngest son of one of Key West's earliest Bahamian settlers. It was completed around 1866. Its oldest part is the kitchen, which was originally used as living quarters while the main house was being built. Its floor plan, columns and pedimented attic show the influence of the Greek Revival style, while its two-story porches, shuttered windows and numerous doors reflect its Bahamian heritage.

The house's squared columns support the porch and a projecting attic level. Typical of structures in low-lying Key West, its ground floor is raised and steps lead to its simple, dignified entrance. Lacy designs in the railings on the first- and second-story porches offer a 19th century, stick-style delicacy that contrasts with the severity of the house's Greek elements and the practicality of its Bahamian aspects.

The interior of the tall, narrow Gideon Lowe House has been decorated in a light-toned, modern style that emphasizes its graceful staircase, Dade County pine plank floors and open beams. Floors are covered with Oriental and rag rugs. The historic house is furnished with many antiques.

The Gideon Lowe House is at 409 Williams St., Key West. Room rates vary seasonally. For further information, from Florida call (305) 294-5702; from outside Florida call (800) 634-8230.

LOUIE'S BACKYARD

The two-story, frame house that is now Louie's Backyard restaurant was built around 1900 for Capt. James Randall Adams. He was a wrecker who made a fortune salvaging goods from ships destroyed off Key West.

During his lifetime, it's said, Adams boasted that everything that went into the home, including its front and side verandas on both levels and its Doric columns, was merchandise that had been salvaged.

Adams' gracious, Dade County pine house was built in the Classical Revival style, with a tin roof, 10 rooms and ceilings 12 feet high. Its kitchen — like others in Key West and in Florida in general — was in a building separate from the rest of the house. This was so that heat and the danger of fire would be kept as far as possible from the living quarters. A narrow porch on the back, along with the porches on the front and sides, allowed cooling breezes to enter windows left open during showers and shaded the walls from the sun.

The residence stayed in the Adams family for a number of years. It then changed hands several times before 1971, when it was purchased by Frances and Louie Signorelli, who opened the patio, living room and dining room into a small restaurant known as Louie's Backyard. That Louie's seated about 20, had one waiter and operated out of a cigar box cash register.

In 1983, Phil and Pat Penney and Proal Perry bought the house from the Signorellis. They renovated the house and doubled the dining space. They also opened the upstairs as the Cafe at Louie's Backyard.

Today's Louie's Backyard includes a large dining room addition, enlarged terrace and high, modern windows on its first and second floors. The renovated house is listed on the National Register of Historic Places.

Louie's Backyard is at 700 Waddell Ave. in Key West. It specializes in creative preparation of local seafood. Lunch is from 11:30 p.m. to 3 p.m.; dinner from 6 p.m. to 10:30 p.m. The cafe is open for dinner from 6 p.m. to 11 p.m. For further information, call (305) 294-1061.

FURTHER READING

The following books will be of interest to those who want to read more about the topics touched on in *Florida Historic Homes*.

Florida Architecture and History

Florida's Vanishing Architecture
Beth Dunlop
Pineapple Press

Mizner's Florida: American Resort Architecture
Donald Curl
American Monograph Newhouse Series

Tropical Splendor
Hap Hatton
Knopf

Houses of St. Augustine, Fifteen-sixty-five to Eighteen-twenty-one
Albert Manucy
Saint Augustine Historical Society

Wooden Houses of Key West
Sharon Wells and Lawson Little
Historic Key West Preservation Board
Florida Department of State

Orlando History in Architecture
Orlando Historic Preservation Board
City of Orlando
Best Litho Inc.

Florida History

Fifty Feet in Paradise
David Nolan
Harcourt Brace Jovanovich

Florida Under Five Flags
Rembert W. Patrick
University of Florida Press

The Other Florida
Gloria Jahoda
Florida Classics Library

Cross Creek
Marjorie Kinnan Rawlings
Scribner

Guides to Residential Architecture

Identifying American Architecture: A Pictorial Guide to Styles and Terms, 1600-1945
John G. Blumenson
American Association for State and Local History

A Field Guide to American Architecture
Carole Rifkind
Plume

American Architecture Since 1780: A Guide to the Styles
Marcus Whiffen
MIT Press

A Field Guide to American Houses
Virginia and Lee McAlester
Knopf

Restaurant/Bed & Breakfast Hotel Guides

Florida's Historic Restaurants
Dawn O'Brien and Becky Roper Matkov
John F. Blair

A Guide to the Small and Historic Lodgings of Florida
Herb Hiller
Pineapple Press

INDEX

Artist House	120	King-Cromartie House	107
Audubon House Museum	116	Kingsley Plantation	45
Bailey House	43	Koreshan Settlement	85
Banyan House	77	Charles Lavalle House	22
The Barnacle	109	Nannie Lee's Strawberry Mansion	69
Bayboro House	76	Harry P. Leu House	66
Beadel House	35	Louie's Backyard	123
Bonnet House	96	Gideon Lowe House	122
Bradlee-McIntyre House	64	Matheson House	118
Brokaw-McDougall House	33	Alfred B. Maclay State Gardens	30
Cabbage Key Inn and Restaurant	82	Murat House	32
Ca'd'Zan	81	Norment-Parry Inn	67
Casa de Solana	52	Oldest House (Key West)	115
Casa Vecchia	98	Dr. Peck House	50
The Casements	63	E.P. Porcher House	68
Chart House Restaurant	101	Quina House	19
Cigar Workers' Houses	75	Raintree Restaurant	51
The Columns	36	Rawlings House	60
Coral Gables House	106	Scotto's Ristorante Italiano	25
Cracker House	37	St. Augustine's Oldest House	46
Curry Mansion	119	Stranahan House	103
Dorr House	21	Thursby House	62
Dubois House	92	Townsend's Plantation	65
Eaton Lodge	121	Victorian House	53
Eden State Gardens	27	La Vieille Maison	93
Edison Winter Home	83	Vizcaya Museum and Gardens	104
Fernandez-Llambias House	48	Wagner Homestead	99
Gamble Plantation	79	Westcott House	47
Gilbert's Bar House of Refuge	91	Whitehall	94
Gregory House	29	Ximenez-Fatio House	49
Hemingway House	117		
Herlong Mansion Bed & Breakfast	59		
Jamie's French Restaurant	24		
Julee Cottage	23		

OTHER SENTINEL BOOKS

Florida Boating and Watersports Guide
by Max Branyon

Florida Eats 1988
by Chris Sherman

Florida Freshwater Fishing Guide
by Max Branyon

Florida Gardening Guide
by Tom MacCubbin

Florida Home Grown — Landscaping
by Tom MacCubbin

Florida Saltwater Fishing Guide
by Max Branyon

Thought You'd Never Ask Part I
by Dorothy Chapman

Thought You'd Never Ask Part II
by Dorothy Chapman

For information or to obtain a catalog, phone Bethany Mott at (407) 420-5588; or write: *Sentinel Books*, **The Orlando Sentinel**, P.O. Box 1100, Orlando, FL 32802.

RR9310A